THE IMF POLICY PARADIGM

THE IMF POLICY PARADIGM

The Macroeconomics of Stabilization, Structural Adjustment, and Economic Development

Wilfred L. David

332, 15
D24 L

Library of Congress Cataloging in Publication Data

David, Wilfred L.
  The IMF policy paradigm.

  Bibliography: p.
  Includes index.
  1. International Monetary Fund.   2. International
finance.   3. Economic stabilization.   4. Economic
development.   I. Title.
HG3881.5.I58D38 1985   332.1'52   85-6533
ISBN 0-03-004408-1 (alk. paper)

Published in 1985 by Praeger Publishers
CBS Educational and Professional Publishing, a Division of CBS Inc.
521 Fifth Avenue, New York, NY 10175 USA

56789 052 987654321

Printed in the United States of America on acid-free paper

INTERNATIONAL OFFICES

Orders from outside the United States should be sent to the appropriate address listed below. Orders from areas not
listed below should be placed through CBS International Publishing, 383 Madison Ave., New York, NY 10175 USA

Australia, New Zealand
Holt Saunders, Pty. Ltd., 9 Waltham St., Artarmon, N.S.W. 2064, Sydney, Australia

Canada
Holt, Rinehart & Winston of Canada, 55 Horner Ave., Toronto, Ontario, Canada M8Z 4X6

Europe, the Middle East, & Africa
Holt Saunders, Ltd., 1 St. Anne's Road, Eastbourne, East Sussex, England BN21 3UN

Japan
Holt Saunders, Ltd., Ichibancho Central Building, 22-1 Ichibancho, 3rd Floor, Chiyodaku, Tokyo, Japan

Hong Kong, Southeast Asia
Holt Saunders Asia, Ltd., 10 Fl, Intercontinental Plaza, 94 Granville Road, Tsim Sha Tsui East, Kowloon,
Hong Kong

**Manuscript submissions should be sent to the Editorial Director, Praeger Publishers, 521 Fifth Avenue,
New York, NY 10175 USA**

Dedicated
to
Peggy Ann and Wilfred, Jr.

Preface

During the past decade or more, the international community has witnessed a stall in the engine of economic progress of a considerable number of developing nations. With the possible exception of a few small nations in Asia, and a relatively smaller number of what are euphemistically termed "newly industrializing countries," the more or less universal picture that presents itself to the observer is one in which the development process has come to a complete halt.

In the majority of cases, the development path seems to be blocked, or visibility is extremely poor. In some cases, there might have been a slippage in the development gear, or essential parts of the engine are worn and need replacing. In others, there might have been a seizure or total breakdown of the engine. Whatever the true nature of the situation, or its underlying causes, the common denominator is that there is no money available from domestic resources to repair or replace the engine, or even to fuel it in the event that it is restarted.

While the above picture is a stark one, there is evidence to suggest that it is not overdrawn. In general, besides the poor overall economic performance (as measured by indicators such as GNP and balance of payments) a visible state of stagnation and/or deterioration in standards of living and the overall quality of life now seems to define the existence of many. In many parts of the developing world, these conditions are associated with, and reflected by, a variety of disequilibrating forces, including: a stagnation or decline in the buoyancy of traditional production activities; the scarcity of basic production inputs, and/or spare parts for capital equipment and machinery; the unavailability of the food and basic consumption goods, at affordable prices, for the majority of the population; and the lack, or poor quality of, basic social and public services.

These are illustrative examples, and are not meant to be exhaustive. The pertinent issue then becomes one of delineating the constellation of factors that may be responsible for these developments. As pointed out in the body of the study, factors operating in the international environment, beyond the control of the developing countries themselves, as well as internal managerial inefficiencies, are part of the cause. However, there is now a consensus that the energy crises of the 1970s, combined with successive recessions in the developed world, might have heightened the crisis.

As a consequence, the majority of developing countries were forced to borrow extensively in international capital markets in the attempt to maintain past and present standards of living. Given the constraints existing in the international financial environment, the International Monetary Fund (IMF) has had to take on the role of what Gerald Helleiner has dubbed "lender of first resort."

In this context, few would deny that the IMF now ranks among the most powerful institutions in the international political economy. In the eyes of many, it has taken on the role of "minister without portfolio" in the large majority of developing countries, which have been implementing Fund-supported programs. Others are of the view that the policy prescriptions, conditionalities, and performance criteria that the IMF imposes on developing countries are not only too harsh and rigid, but in many cases tend to be based on economic theories that have limited applicability in a development context. One also encounters a much more cynical view that IMF policies are designed to protect the interests of rich international bankers and powerful industrial nations.

On the other hand, some commentators feel that the conditions underlying IMF programs may not be stringent enough, given its relatively limited lending portfolio, the excess demand that exists for its funds, and what is presumed to be internal mismanagement in the developing world. A related claim is that the only hope for economic survival in the majority of borrowing member countries lies in their acceptance and implementation of IMF policy advice, reversing earlier policy mistakes, and putting their domestic economic houses in order.

This study attempts to throw some light on both the theoretical and policy issues surrounding the debate. Its primary focus is on the nature of the economic paradigm that informs the IMF's policy–theoretical thrust, and draws some of the implications for broad-based development. While there is some intrinsic interest in the policies and their implications, we also considered it necessary to present an exposé of the paradigm's analytical foundations and the related policy–theoretical perspectives.

The study originated as an attempt to explain the theoretical foundations of IMF policies to my graduate students. One of their specific concerns was with the relevance of standard textbook macroeconomic theory to the conditions existing in the developing world, and how the underlying principles could be amended, or otherwise integrated with relevant aspects of development theory. However, as the study progressed, the necessity to go beyond theory, and to address questions of policy, as well as their implications for economic development, became particularly obvious.

It is hoped, therefore, that the menu that has emerged, or the relevant parts of it, would be easily digested by a diverse reading public. As such, the study can be used as a teaching tool, either in its own right, or in conjunction with more formal texts. It can also be read with profit by policy analysts, development officials, and others interested in the problems of international development.

Wilfred L. David
Washington, D.C.
February, 1985

Acknowledgments

This study would not have been completed without the considerable assistance received from various sources throughout the years.

The award of a Fulbright Research Professorship during the 1984–85 academic year provided me with ample time to reflect and observe relevant developments in the field. I am thankful to the Council for the International Exchange of Scholars, the Board of Foreign Scholarships, Wayne Peterson, and Terry Blatt of the Office of Academic Programs for their support.

The Principal and Fellows of Linacre College, Oxford University, provided the requisite facilities and a scholarly environment for research, writing, and discussion. Some of my former mentors, including Sir John and Lady Hicks, and Lords Balogh and Robbins, always spared time to discuss pertinent issues, although they did not necessarily share all of my views.

The author therefore cannot claim a proprietary right to the words and ideas expressed herein. The study also draws heavily on the published or unpublished ideas of a large number of colleagues and friends both inside the World Bank and the IMF, as well as from views expressed by scholars and government officials. In this case, it is hoped that the customary general statement of indebtedness would be accepted.

Nevertheless, special mention must be made of a few individuals who have supported my efforts over the years, or who have otherwise discussed portions of the study with me. These include Graham Donaldson, Peter Hopcraft, Jean Curling, Aubrey Williams, Alfredo Sfeir-Younis, Marius Veeraart, Pat Cacho and Bill Cuddihy of the World Bank; and several members of the Fund's research department.

I am also deeply grateful to my editors: Barbara Leffel, Stephanie Grant, Mia Crowley, and David Stebbing for the time and care devoted to overseeing the production of this work.

Of course, none of the above-mentioned individuals should be held responsible for the views expressed in the study, or for any errors or omissions.

Last, but by no means least, I am thankful to my wife, Peggy Ann David, and my son, Wilfred, Jr., for their constant and unselfish support. This study is dedicated to them as a small token of my gratitude.

Contents

List of Tables

THE IMF POLICY PARADIGM

PART I

SETTING THE SCENE

1
Introduction

Over the past decade, the international community has become increasingly aware of the growing incidence of the internal and external disequilibria that continue to plague the developing nations of the world, especially the poorest. As is now well known, these imbalances are reflected in the congruence of several factors, including: (1) large and escalating balance-of-payments deficits, and the possibility that these are neither temporary nor self-reversing; (2) increasing financial dependency as evidenced by the worsening of external debt and reserve positions; (3) stagnation and worsening of aggregate growth and employment rates, and, in some cases, a visible retrogression in the overall development process; and (4) accelerating inflation. These problems have become much more evident and acute since the oil shocks of 1973–74 and 1979–80, and are particularly pressing for the non–oil-exporting developing countries.

The interplay of the above-mentioned factors has resulted in an increasing demand for liquidity by the developing nations. In general, such liquidity can be derived from their own reserve holdings of gold and foreign exchange, as well as from fast disbursing loans from commercial and official sources. However, the majority of these countries have limited gold and other foreign exchange reserve holdings, and their ability to build up these reserves has been severely weakened by successive international recessions. For the large majority, gross international reserves cover only a few months, and even weeks, of import requirements. Account should also be taken of the opportunity cost of holding excessive international reserves. The higher such reserve holdings, the less is the ability of countries to finance their development effort from their own resources (Helleiner 1983).

Another factor of importance is that the amount of liquidity available from commercial bank loans to these countries has proved to be limited. A few countries (e.g., India, China, Mexico, and Zaire) have been considered creditworthy by commercial bankers, based on perceptions about mineral

3

and other resource and marketing potentials. However, the larger majority of low-income countries are still considered "credit risks" by the international banking community. As a result, loans to these countries typically include high-risk premiums, and have therefore proved to be much more expensive than the average for developing countries in general.

The worsening liquidity situation and the relatively high costs of commercial loans have forced developing countries to make extensive use of the liquidity provided by multilateral credit agencies such as the International Monetary Fund (IMF). While IMF credits to its developing-country members have reached new peak levels, funds from these sources still finance less than 10 percent of their combined balance-of-payments deficits. Nevertheless, the IMF's overall international influence is much more significant than its aggregate lending profile suggests. Acceptance of IMF programs has now become a necessary prerequisite for other forms of external finance. Most commercial bankers place a considerable store on the ability of developing nations to successfully negotiate IMF loans. There is also growing evidence of a positive correlation between acceptance of IMF lending conditions and the ability of developing countries to successfully negotiate official loans from major industrial lenders.

According to recent public statements made by the managing director and other senior officials of the IMF, several countries (e.g., Yugoslavia, Kenya, Somalia, and Ghana) have been able to achieve some degree of success in pursuing the short-term stabilization goals stipulated under Fund-supported programs. The basis of this claim is that government authorities in these countries, by following IMF policy advice, have been able to reverse earlier policy mistakes, thereby restoring economic growth and laying the foundations for future economic survival.

This optimistic assessment has received corroboration from the results of several studies by IMF staff analysts (Reichmann and Stillson 1978; Donovan 1982; Kelly 1982). In general, these studies conclude that countries that undertook Fund-supported programs in the 1970s were able to achieve significant reductions in their aggregate domestic inflation rates, compared to other developing countries that did not pursue such programs. An additional contention is that these adjustments generally were not achieved at the expense of lower growth and consumption rates.

Despite these developments, there is still a heated academic and policy debate about the nature and consequences of programs supported by the IMF. The underlying issues are multifaceted, and cover the spectrum of theoretical, practical policy, social, and political considerations. This study focuses primarily on certain theoretical and policy underpinnings, and their implications for broad-based development and structural transformation in the developing countries. The relevant issues are of course closely tied to more practical ones of political economy, and these cannot be ignored. The latter revolve around the economic, political, and social costs of IMF programs in relation to the overall benefits that are supposed to ensue.

In the above context, it can be hypothesized that there is usually a symbiotic relationship between theory and policy, even though a one-to-one correspondence is not always encountered in practice. While the theoretical and policy foundations of IMF programs are by no means monolithic, a reasonable working hypothesis is that there tends to be a high degree of correspondence between certain preferred theoretical frameworks and the policy advice meted out to the developing countries.

To the extent that it is possible to identify the unique features of the policy–theoretical framework that guides IMF-supported programs, meaningful questions can be asked about the validity of the theoretical and empirical generalizations on which they are based, as well as their realism and relevance in a development context. These and related questions are considered important since the supporting body of theoretical and empirical generalizations usually forms the basis for IMF policy diagnoses, objectives, and targets.

While there will continue to be disagreements about the criteria that should be used to assess the IMF policy–theoretical framework and its supporting theoretical and empirical generalizations, this study takes as a point of departure the particular world view or paradigm on which they are based. Accordingly, it is necessary to locate this framework within the much wider context of intellectual history and the sociology of knowledge, that is, within systems of knowledge and ideas that have become dominant over time.

THE PARADIGM OR WORLD VIEW

The notion of a paradigm is by no means a clear-cut one, and both economists and philosophers find it controversial. In its most general sense, however, a paradigm represents a set of shared intellectual commitments that help to shape our perceptions about social and economic reality. It provides the intellectual framework for the study of such reality, defines the sets of problems that are considered worthy of investigation, and delineates the requisite sets of criteria for judging the appropriateness of answers to such problems. Such an intellectual framework is typically governed by a world view or ideology together with supporting sets of theories, policies, methodological approaches, and research programs.

During the course of intellectual history, there has emerged an impressive body of thought drawing attention to the fact that social scientists operate as "sociological groups," defined by similarities in life styles, social locations, philosophies of life, intellectual perspectives, and value judgments which they make about social and economic reality. According to Schumpeter (1949, 1978), the cohesion and "corporate spirit" associated with such group membership, while facilitating the accumulation of theoretical and factual knowledge, nevertheless produces a mind-frame that becomes increasingly conservative and resistant to change. However, he was careful to draw a distinction between social science as a technique "that develops in a social group professionally devoted to its cultivation" on the one hand, and "the ideological aspects of methods and the results that emerge from the scientific activities of such a group."

Schumpeter's view is that the social mechanism is a source of "ideology," and represents a pre- and extra-scientific "vision" of the socioeconomic process and social reality. It is this vision that is subjected to scientific treatment and loses the force of ideology once it is subjected to scientific testing and analysis. As he states:

> Analytical work begins with material provided by our vision of things and that vision is ideological almost by definition. It embodies the picture of things as we see them, and whether there is any possible motive for wishing to see them in a given rather than in another light, the way in which we see things can hardly be distinguished from the way in which we wish to see them. (1949, p. 42)

In this context, ideologies are "not simply lies," but may represent truthful statements of what a person thinks he or she sees. One conclusion that emerges from Schumpeter's perspective is that the practice of scientific activity per se does not require that we divest ourselves of our value judgments, group interests, or commitments. The real issue, however, is whether scientists (economists) are willing to make explicit their value judgments and, in a much wider context, reveal the intellectual biases that may be associated with certain group affiliations.

Schumpeter's ideas can also be used as a means of identifying features of a well-developed paradigm. There are at least three such readily identifiable features. First, a specific "community of scholars," "scientific group," or "invisible college" normally coalesces around it. Second, it usually has a distinct cognitive structure which reflects the shared values, epistemological beliefs, and modes of analysis to which the scientific community (of economists and social scientists) subscribes. Third, it tends to be associated with, and is usually transmitted through, well-respected research traditions and academic programs. These and related features of a well-developed and dominant paradigm usually make it extremely difficult to overthrow, even in the face of strong challenges from the outside.

It goes without saying that the policy–theoretical frameworks underlying IMF lending programs are synergistic with the orthodox paradigm of economics and economic development. While no formal defense of this proposition is provided here, it is supported by the fact that IMF policy prescriptions reveal a heavy reliance on, and a marked preference for, orthodox theories, economic philosophies, and analytical modes. In this context, it should be noted that the IMF approach is an eclectic one, and draws its substance from various combinations of neoclassical, Keynesian, and monetarist world views. Some perspectives of thought underlying these pillars of orthodox economics are illustrated in Table 1.1

These world views are also replicated in the field of economic development. It has been suggested that the IMF is essentially an "adjustment" institution, that is, it is concerned with lending for short-term programs of stabilization and adjustment. Contextually, it is usually distinguished from other multilateral agencies like the World Bank which are essentially concerned with the longer-term problems of development. While this distinction has remained historically true, it has become more and more tenuous. First, Fund-supported programs take on a much longer-term perspective, and at times call for substantial reordering of the development priorities of borrowing member countries. Second, and in analytical terms, there is always a necessary connection between the requirements of short-term stabilization and adjustment vis-à-vis those of longer-term structural change and development. This becomes evident if development is viewed as an adaptive and historical process, rather than in terms of a rational and logical continuum involving discrete time periods of varying duration.

Even if the IMF is not considered a "development" institution its programs can be meaningfully assessed from a developmental perspective. Besides the reasons mentioned above, these programs have come to have serious consequences for the lives of billions of people living in the developing world. From this perspective, it is possible to identify certain "paradigmatic" tenets that have been traditionally associated with orthodox development economics, and which, it is hypothesized, support the analytical pillars undergirding the IMF lending approach. Table 1.2 presents a schematized framework of the principles on which the orthodox paradigm of economic development are based. A brief elaboration is provided below.

A first is the widespread belief that there are certain universal factors that affect total or per capita income growth (for example, capital accumulation, savings, and industrialization), and that the extent to which the latter factors can promote growth is also a function of certain universal principles. One set of principles is concerned with resource mobilization based on the assumption of a direct relationship between investment and national output and income. The basic principle is therefore one that stresses rapid accumulation to facilitate macroeconomic growth, as well as acceleration, that is, that there should be a structure that allows for rapid economic growth. In this regard, it is also postulated that the possibilities for rapid mobilization are, in the majority of cases, constrained by a variety of resource gaps and pivotal scarcities, including: capital, savings, foreign

Table 1.1 *Keynesian political economy and its rivals*

	Radical–Heterodox	*Neo-Keynesian (post-Keynesian)*	*Keynesian*	*Neo-Classical (post-Keynesian)*	*Monetarist–New Classical (post-Keynesian)*
Microeconomic Base	Monopoly capitalism	Imperfect markets	Imperfect markets	Perfect markets	Perfect markets
Money	Buttresses power structure	Accommodates real economic changes	Interacts with real economy very intimately	Money and all other things important	Only money matters
Inflation	Structural; due to excessive profits	Due to changes in profit margins and money wages	Due to aggregate demand pressures	Due to Phillips curve tradeoff in short run; money supply and portfolio changes in long run	Primarily a monetary phenomenon
Employment	Full employment creates capitalist crises	Growth with full employment desirable	Underemployment equilibrium though full employment desirable	Full employment equilibrium always assumed	"Natural rate of unemployment"
Distribution	Most important issues; labor exploitation	Determined by institutional factors	Not important	Determined by marginal productivity and laws of supply and demand	
Ideology	Extreme left	Left	Center	Right of center	Extreme right
Protagonists	Marxists, Galbraith, Bowles, Gintis	Robinson, Kaldor, Eichner, Kregel	Harrod, Weintraub, Davidson	Samuelson, Hicks, Solow, Tobin	Friedman, Phelps, Meltzer, Brunner

Source: Compiled by author.

8

Table 1.2 *The orthodox paradigm of economic development*

Analysis and method	*Models and theories*	*Goals and values*
Rationalism	Neoclassical	Economic growth
Positivism	Keynesian	Price stability
Economism	Monetarist	Balance-of-payments
Equilibrium	Rational expectations	equilibrium
		Fiscal discipline
Development processes	*Global structure*	*Policy thrust*
Trickle down and	Integration and	Market orientation
diffusion	interdependence	Minimal state
Capital accumulation	Global harmony	Price and material
Resource mobilization	Free trade	incentives
Managerial efficiency	International resource	Incrementalism
	transfers	

Source: Compiled by author.

exchange, and skills. It is also posited that the removal of these constraints requires the encouragement and establishment of capitalist-type institutions, which are considered to have built-in incentives for promoting individual growth, innovation, and related developmental attributes.

A second principle is that of sacrifice based on the widespread assumption of resource scarcity relative to human wants. Given scarce resources, it is impossible to satisfy all of society's goals simultaneously. This means that resources have to be efficiently utilized if material gains are to be maximized. A further assumption is that the realization of optimal material gains will inevitably lead to their equitable distribution. The basis of this assumption is that the resources that are employed receive rewards that are commensurate with the intensity with which they are used, and, in general, their respective contributions to increases in material output. As economists argue, sacrifice requires rational choice in the allocation of scarce resources. One implication is that if the alternatives presented are not rationally chosen, resource scarcity is likely to increase with the passage of time, with negative consequences for living standards and economic growth. The economist's decision rule is that prices should equal real costs in all commodity and factor markets, both nationally and internationally.

A third principle is that, given society's objectives and the means identified to achieve them, there should be some mechanism for translating the preferences of the population into society's objectives. In this context, orthodoxy gives primacy of place to the market mechanism, on the assumption that there is some consistency between private decisions as expressed in the marketplace and the larger public good. This world view is supported by an implicit theory of political behavior in which politicians and government bureaucrats are considered to be well-informed guardians of the public welfare.

A fourth principle is based on a preferred interest in a liberal world environment governed by free trade and exchange as the most favored development strategy. This is merely an extension of the market ideology to the international arena. The same normative forces are seen as operating both intranationally and internationally, with the private market viewed as the most efficient and effective mechanism for allocating and distributing resources. As is well known, this philosophy is predicated on the requirements of international specialization, patterns of trade based on comparative advantage, and the equitable distribution of the gains from trade and exchange based on free trade and the free international flow of resources.

The above analytical pillars of developmental orthodoxy tend to lend support, in one way or another, to an all-embracing methodological and ideological thrust in which development is conceptualized as a rational process governed by certain universal laws of change. The process is also considered to be a gradual, harmonious, and mechanical one of adjustment in a world of perfect equilibrium. As indicated earlier, the process is assumed to be driven by prices and markets whose behavior minimizes conflict and ensures that development benefits all groups, both nationally and internationally.

As eloquently described by two development economists:

> The ruling paradigm of the economics of development rests on the classical–neoclassical view of the world in which change is gradual, marginalist, non-disruptive, equilibrating, and largely painless. Incentives are the bedrock of economic growth. Once initiated, growth becomes automatic and all-pervasive, spreading among nations and trickling down among classes so that everybody benefits from the process. This view is analogous to the communicating vessels of elementary hydraulics; the pressure of the vessel with higher initial endowments leads to raising the water level in the other vessels. The mechanism that trips off change and restores equilibrium is the pressure created by non-identical endowments. The impulse is transmitted through the pipeline that connects the vessels. Analogously, development is initiated by incentives arising from inequality and is promoted by the market mechanisms that connect the rich and the poor. According to this paradigm, therefore, what is required for development is to create the proper incentives, to perfect the market mechanisms, and thereby to initiate the changes that lead to self-propelled take-offs. The incurable optimistic payoff is the general spread of development and the homogenization of the rich and the poor to the extent that they become indistinguishable. (Nugent and Yotopolous 1979, p. 542)

The debate on the nature of orthodox development principles is a far-reaching one. Some pertinent areas of concern are highlighted throughout this volume, especially in Chapters 8 and 9. However, several commentators on the subject believe that some of the basic tenets of developmental orthodoxy should be amended if they are to meaningfully reflect the real problems of development and underdevelopment (Lewis 1984; Streeten 1974; Nugent and Yotopolous 1979; David 1984).

At this point, it can be commented that the IMF, under its Articles of Agreement, is mandated to promote a liberal world environment. Its policy prescriptions reveal a distinct preference for free market solutions to the problems of stabilization and development. As detailed in other parts of the study, the trade, output and factor pricing, and exchange rate policies that it advocates are based on the idea that market prices reflect scarcities, and reliance on them would lead, by and large, to efficient (correct) allocative, distributive, and growth decisions. This philosophy is also synergistic with the Fund's insistence in its programs on macroeconomic, fiscal, and monetary discipline as a means of promoting noninflationary growth, efficiency, price stability, and balance-of-payments equilibrium.

ORGANIZATION OF THIS STUDY

The study is subdivided into four major parts. Part I sets the scene, outlines the study's focus, and provides a brief overview of the IMF's lending approach as mandated by its Articles of Agreement. The principles of conditionality governing its loans and the performance criteria that have to be met by borrowers are also discussed. The complementarity between IMF and World Bank policies is also highlighted in terms of the relationship between short-term aggregate demand management on the one hand, and longer-term structural adjustment and supply management, on the other.

The main analytical foundations of the IMF policy paradigm are outlined and discussed in Parts II and III. In Part II, the primary focus is on the analysis of orthodox demand management as based on Keynesian-type income-expenditure models and monetarist approaches to stabilization and adjustment. In Part III, the emphasis shifts to issues in the area of supply management, and the related requirements for medium and longer-term structural change. This is an area in which there seems to be an increasing similarity between the economic philosophies of the IMF and the World Bank.

Thus, while the emphasis in Part II is mainly on *stabilization*, (theories and policies concerned with the restoration of macroeconomic equilibrium in the face of various types of disequilibria) the primary concern in Part III is with *liberalization* (theories and policies dealing with questions of resource allocation and the role of various types of prices). Attention is drawn to the nature of price and other "distortions" that define the trade and exchange regimes of developing countries, as well as the policies that are advocated for their removal. These are essentially policies designed to liberalize markets for goods, factors of production, and foreign exchange.

The discussion in Part IV focuses on three interrelated sets of issues. Some of these revolve around the burden of adjustment, and the relative emphasis that should be placed on external and internal factors in explaining the various imbalances facing developing countries. In the typical case, IMF policy prescriptions are based on diagnoses that view internal excesses as the primary cause of such disequilibria. By contrast, some analysts argue that such difficulties are traceable, in the main, to exogenous variations in the demand for and supply of primary commodities. To the extent that this is true, the balance of payments and other disequilibria facing the developing world are primarily a reflection of the industrial and trading structure of countries, and not necessarily the over-expansionary demand and/or inappropriate supply management policies.

Another set of issues revolves around the potential conflicts between the goals and targets underlying short-term macroeconomic stabilization and the more fundamental goals of development: employment, income distribution, poverty alleviation, and the fulfillment of basic human needs. Those developing countries attempting to meet these goals must often reorient their domestic development priorities and related public investment strategies in order to satisfy the conditionalities underlying IMF-supported programs. Some would argue that IMF conditionalities are not harsh enough and that, whatever the nature of long-term development goals, the only hope for the continued economic survival of many developing countries lies in their changing course, thereby reversing past and present internal excesses and inefficiencies.

A final question concerns the nature of development strategies, and, in particular, whether the attainment of broad-based development and structural transformation can be meaningfully achieved through the use of market-oriented, monetarist, and free trade policies. Related to this is a question concerning the optimal role of the state vis-à-vis the private sector in the development process, and the criteria that should be used in demarcating their respective roles.

2

IMF Lending Policy: An Overview

The broad framework specifying the conditions under which the IMF lends to its member countries is set out in its Articles of Agreement. The fundamental purposes were made explicit in the original Articles of Agreement which established the Fund in 1944, and they have been more or less upheld in the two amendments in the basic charter which were made in 1969 and 1978.

MANDATE AND LENDING RESOURCES

From the perspective of this study, the best reference point is provided by Article 1, which lists six broad purposes of the Fund, as follows: (1) the promotion of international monetary cooperation; (2) the expansion of balanced growth and international trade; (3) the promotion of exchange stability, the maintenance of orderly exchange arrangements, and the avoidance of competitive exchange depreciation; (4) the establishment of multilateral payments systems; (5) the correction of balance-of-payments maladjustments; and (6) the provision of resources to lessen the degree of such disequilibria.

The overall philosophy stresses the maintenance of a liberal world economic and financial environment, which promotes financial and economic cooperation among member countries, the objective being to facilitate the expansion and balanced growth of world trade. The aims of such cooperation still remain the attainment and maintenance of high levels of employment and real incomes within each member country, through the development of the productive resources of all members. It was envisaged that these aims would be best attained in the context of a multilateral payments system that fosters orderly trade and exchange stability, and one in which payments imbalances can be redressed without resort to measures that run counter to national and international prosperity. This philosophy is in the tradition of orthodox economic thinking in which orderly trade and exchange are considered to be two of the most effective weapons for guaranteeing international equilibrium and for diffusing international development.

This comes out in bolder relief when the purposes stated in Articles 1(II) and 1(V) are considered. According to Article 1(II), a primary purpose of the Fund is to "facilitate the expansion and balanced growth of international trade and to contribute thereby to the promotion and maintenance of high levels of employment and real incomes and to the development of the productive resources of all members as primary objectives of economic policy." Article 1(V) states: "to give confidence to members by making the Fund's resources temporarily available to them under adequate safeguards, and providing opportunity to correct maladjustments in their balance of payments without resorting to measures destructive of national or international stability."

Article 1(II) places emphasis on the "balanced expansion of international trade" in the context of a liberal world environment, free from various forms of protectionism. It also links the balanced growth of international trade to the expansion of real incomes and employment. Free trade is therefore seen as providing the major "engine of growth," with interdependence among trading partners at all levels providing a stimulus to the expansion of output, incomes, and employment. There is a general developmental tone in Article 1(II), though perhaps not in the more fundamental sense discussed in Chapter 9 of this study.

Article 1(V) emphasizes the fact that a primary purpose of the Fund is the correction of balance-of-payments maladjustments. Several types of payments disequilibria can be identified, with the nature of the corrective action recommended depending on the specific type. In a general sense, however, such disequilibria are reflected by a situation in which the current account deficit is in excess of sustainable capital flows from all sources. When this occurs, IMF loans are supposed to help member countries overcome their balance-of-payments problems, as well as to maintain a sustainable payments position for some reasonable period ahead.

Article 1(V) also states that efforts to correct the payments disequilibria should be undertaken "without resorting to measures destructive of national and international prosperity." At one level, this can be interpreted to mean that countries should avoid using policy measures that are likely to result in major disruptions in economic and social life. At another level, it implies that individual countries, in pursuing their chosen policy objectives, should not disturb unduly the policies of other countries with different policy objectives. To the extent that countries are able to strike the correct balance between the competing objectives of independence for national policies and the resource gains from international integration, both national and international economic welfare would be optimized.

The Fund's Articles of Agreement also envisage a pivotal role for the exchange rate regime in terms of the broader objectives of the international financial and economic system, that is, the balance-of-payments adjustment process, the promotion of balanced world trade, and the expansion of employment and real incomes. As stated in Article 1, the exchange rate should be as stable as possible, and countries should avoid competitive exchange rate depreciations. The need for member countries to promote a stable and orderly exchange rate system has been given renewed emphasis in a new Article IV which was introduced under the second amendment to the Articles of Agreement. The Fund is now required to carry out surveillance of the exchange rate policies of its members to ensure that: (1) there are no unfair competitive manipulations of exchange rates; and (2) exchange rate adjustments are as smooth as possible in order to minimize the destabilizing effects of short-term capital movements, and in order to avoid the relatively sharp cost effects and resource shifts that are likely to accompany large forced movements in exchange rates. Some other issues surrounding exchange rate adjustment are taken up in Chapter 7.

We now briefly outline the nature of IMF lending facilities that are used to achieve the broad purposes set out in the Articles of Agreement. At the outset, it should be noted that the International Monetary Fund, as the name signifies, was set up as a "fund" or "pool" of currencies and gold subscribed to by member countries. These subscriptions are made in proportion to their quotas, which are determined by economic criteria and political forces that define status of members in the global political economy.

As indicated in Table 2.1, the combined quotas of IMF members amount to approximately 89.2 billion Special Drawing Rights (SDRs). The value of the SDR is about 1.1 U.S. dollars. The quotas are closely related to: (1) members' subscription to the IMF; (2) their drawing rights under regular and special facilities; (3) their voting power; and (4) their share of any allocation of SDRs (discussed below). Every member of the IMF is required to subscribe an amount equal to its quota, and an amount not exceeding 25 percent of this quota has to be paid in reserve assets. The remainder is paid in a member's own currency. A member's voting power is determined by 250 "basic votes" plus one vote for each 100,000 SDRs subscribed as quota (IMF 1984).

These quota subscriptions now constitute the main source of the IMF's financial assistance to its members. The Articles of Agreement have provided for a general review of quotas every five years, and periodic increases in such quotas have resulted from no less than seven general reviews. However, the general consensus is that these quota increases have failed to catch up with the expansion of international transactions, so that quotas increasingly represent only a small and declining proportion of the payments imbalances facing member countries.

Table 2.1 Quotas and voting power of Fund members

Member	Quotas (million SDRs)	Quota Shares (percent of total)	Member	Quotas (million SDRs)	Quota Shares (percent of total)	Member	Quotas (million SDRs)	Quota Shares (percent of total)
Afghanistan	86.7	0.10	Guinea	57.9	0.06	Philippines	440.4	0.49
Algeria	623.1	0.70	Guinea-Bissau	7.5	0.01	Portugal	376.6	0.42
Antigua and Barbuda	5.0	0.01	Guyana	49.2	0.06	Qatar	114.9	0.13
Argentina	1,113.0	1.25	Haiti	44.1	0.05	Romania	523.4	0.59
Australia	1,619.2	1.81	Honduras	67.8	0.08	Rwanda	43.8	0.05
Austria	775.6	0.87	Hungary	530.7	0.59	St. Christopher and Nevis	4.5	0.01
Bahamas	66.4	0.07	Iceland	59.6	0.07	St. Lucia	7.5	0.01
Bahrain	48.9	0.05	India	2,207.7	2.47	St. Vincent	4.0	0.004
Bangladesh	287.5	0.32	Indonesia	1,009.7	1.13	São Tomé and Principe	4.0	0.004
Barbados	34.1	0.04	Iran, Islamic Rep. of	660.0	0.74	Saudi Arabia	3,202.4	3.59
Belgium	2,080.4	2.33	Iraq	504.0	0.56	Senegal	85.1	0.10
Belize	9.5	0.01	Ireland	343.4	0.38	Seychelles	3.0	0.003
Benin	31.3	0.04	Israel	446.6	0.50	Sierra Leone	57.9	0.06
Bhutan	2.5	0.002	Italy	2,909.1	3.26	Singapore	92.4	0.10
Bolivia	90.7	0.10	Ivory Coast	165.5	0.19	Solomon Islands	5.0	0.01
Botswana	22.1	0.02	Jamaica	145.5	0.16	Somalia	44.2	0.05
Brazil	1,461.3	1.64	Japan	4,223.3	4.73	South Africa	915.7	1.03
Burkina Faso	31.6	0.04	Jordan	73.9	0.08	Spain	1,286.0	1.44
Burma	137.0	0.15	Kampuchea, Democratic	25.0	0.03	Sri Lanka	223.1	0.25
Burundi	42.7	0.05	Kenya	142.0	0.16	Sudan	169.7	0.19
Cameroon	92.7	0.10	Korea	462.8	0.52	Suriname	49.3	0.06
Canada	2,941.0	3.30	Kuwait	635.3	0.71	Swaziland	24.7	0.03
Cape Verde	4.5	0.01	Lao People's Dem. Rep.	29.3	0.03	Sweden	1,064.3	1.19
Central African Rep.	30.4	0.03	Lebanon	78.7	0.09	Syrian Arab Rep.	139.1	0.16
Chad	30.6	0.03	Lesotho	15.1	0.02	Tanzania	107.0	0.12
Chile	440.5	0.49	Liberia	71.3	0.08	Thailand	386.6	0.43
China	2,390.9	2.68				Togo	38.4	0.04
Colombia	394.2	0.44						

Table 2.1 (Continued)

Member	Quotas (million SDRs)	Quota Shares (percent of total)	Member	Quotas (million SDRs)	Quota Shares (percent of total)	Member	Quotas (million SDRs)	Quota Shares (percent of total)
Comoros	4.5	0.01	Libya	515.7	0.58	Trinidad and Tobago	170.1	0.19
Congo, People's Rep. of	37.3	0.04	Luxembourg	77.0	0.09	Tunisia	138.2	0.15
Costa Rica	84.1	0.09	Madagascar	66.4	0.07	Turkey	429.1	0.48
Cyprus	69.7	0.08	Malawi	37.2	0.04	Uganda	99.6	0.11
Denmark	711.0	0.80	Malaysia	550.6	0.62	United Arab Emirates	202.6	0.24
Djibouti	8.0	0.01	Maldives	2.0	0.002	United Kingdom	6,194.0	6.94
Dominica	4.0	0.004	Mali	50.8	0.06	United States	17,918.3	20.08
Dominican Rep.	112.1	0.13	Malta	45.1	0.05	Uruguay	163.8	0.18
Ecuador	150.7	0.17	Mauritania	33.9	0.04	Vanuatu	9.0	0.01
Egypt	463.4	0.52	Mauritius	53.6	0.06	Venezuela	1,371.5	1.54
El Salvador	89.0	0.10	Mexico	1,165.5	1.31	Viet Nam	176.8	0.20
Equatorial Guinea	18.4	0.02	Morocco	306.6	0.34	Western Samoa	6.0	0.01
Ethiopia	70.6	0.08	Nepal	37.3	0.04	Yemen Arab Rep.	43.3	0.05
Fiji	36.5	0.04	Netherlands	2,264.8	2.46	Yemen, People's Dem. Rep. of	77.2	0.09
Finland	574.9	0.64	New Zealand	461.6	0.52	Yugoslavia	613.0	0.69
France	4,482.8	5.02	Nicaragua	68.2	0.08	Zaire	291.0	0.33
Gabon	73.1	0.08	Niger	33.7	0.04	Zambia	270.3	0.30
Gambia, The	17.1	0.02	Nigeria	849.5	0.95	Zimbabwe	191.0	0.21
Germany, Fed. Rep. of	5,403.7	6.06	Norway	699.0	0.78	Total	89,240.8	100.0[1]
Ghana	204.5	0.23	Oman	63.1	0.07			
Greece	399.9	0.45	Pakistan	546.3	0.61			
Grenada	6.0	0.01	Panama	102.2	0.11			
Guatemala	108.0	0.12	Papua New Guinea	65.9	0.07			
			Paraguay	48.4	0.05			
			Peru	330.9	0.37			

[1]The sum of the individual percentage shares differs from 100.0 because of rounding.

Source: IMF 1984.

Note: 1 SDR is equal to 1.1 U.S. dollar approximately.

The quotas bear little relation to member demands for liquidity, and, as indicated above, are more reflective of the economic and political bargaining strength of respective members. As a result, many developing countries contend that the policies governing quota allocations do not sufficiently reflect the true nature of their trading and industrial structure, for example, their relatively high commodity and partner concentration of trade, and the trade instability that they frequently encounter.

The general argument is that quota allocations tend to be inversely related to the liquidity needs of developing countries. A kind of asymmetry has emerged in which countries with relatively high national incomes and reserve holdings have greater access to the Fund's financial resources, compared to the poorer ones whose *need* for such resources tends to be much greater. A more egalitarian formula for fixing quotas would undoubtedly result in larger allocations to the developing countries, with minimal dislocations to their more developed counterparts. This is important for another reason alluded to in the previous chapter. Developing countries generally have low gold and foreign reserve holdings, and their access to commercial loans tends to be limited. Where adequate liquidity is not provided by institutions like the IMF, they have been forced to use the more high-cost, relatively short-term credit available from private commercial sources. The result has been a worsening of their debt service problems.

The types of borrowing permitted from IMF resources are subdivided into four equal tranches. The first, initially known as the Gold Tranche, is now called the Reserve Tranche. When a country draws on this tranche, it is merely withdrawing the currency it deposited with the IMF as part of its membership subscription. The other tranches are known as Credit Tranches. Drawing on these tranches normally involves the purchase of another member's currency (i.e., foreign exchange) in exchange for the currency of the borrowing member. This, in effect, constitutes a loan from the IMF.

The first of the tranches (the First Credit Tranche) is available on easier terms than the other three (termed Higher Credit Tranches). Drawings on the First Credit Tranche are permitted when, in the Fund's view, the members concerned are making "reasonable efforts" to correct their balance-of-payments problem. By contrast, drawings under the high-credit tranches usually require substantial justification by borrowing members that they are making "strong efforts" to overcome their balance-of-payments difficulties. Resources under these higher-credit tranches are normally provided under stand-by credits, which are based on the observance of very rigid performance criteria and require drawings in installments.

Since the 1960s, and especially since the 1970s, IMF financial resources have been augmented substantially through the addition of several new lending facilities, including: the Compensatory Financing facility (created in 1963), the Buffer Stock Financing facility, the Oil facility

(1974-76), the Trust Fund (1977), and the Extended Fund facility (1979). The latter was replaced by an Enlarged Access Policy in 1981. The Oil facility and the Trust Fund are no longer in existence. A point of emphasis, however, is that the addition of these new facilities has resulted in substantial increases in the use of Fund resources in recent years. This is shown in Table 2.2

In addition, the IMF activated a Special Drawing Rights (SDR) facility in 1970 as an alternative source of reserve creation by its members. Its creation grew out of a concern over the adequacy of international liquidity. Some economists even saw the facility as a means of achieving greater international monetary integration, more symmetry in the international monetary system, and the eventual conversion of the IMF into a world central bank. The dust has not yet settled in the debate surrounding the potential role of the SDR facility. One burning issue, however, continues to center around the basis on which SDRs are allocated to IMF members. Since SDRs are allocated in relation to membership quotas, the underlying issue is similar to that raised with respect to the factors governing quota allocations.

To the extent that SDRs are allocated on the basis of members' quota subscriptions, they reflect, by and large, the economic and bargaining strength of IMF members rather than their need for reserves. As in the case of quotas, SDR allocations have shown a bias in favor of countries with large reserves and convertible currencies. This has resulted in several proposals for revising the quota and SDR allocation system. These include proposals for increasing the size of quotas, divorcing access to SDRs and other IMF facilities from their dependence on the size of quotas, and the allocation of a larger proportion of SDRs to developing countries by introducing some form of SDR/aid link. For a further discussion, see Bird (1979).

CONDITIONALITY AND THE ADJUSTMENT PROCESS

Article 1(V) of the Fund's Articles of Agreement states that the use of the agency's resources should be made available to member countries on a temporary basis and under "adequate safeguards." These "safeguards" reflect certain "conditionalities" that the Fund usually wishes to see a member follow in order for the latter to have access to the Fund's resources. In other words, conditionality refers to the safeguards the IMF is required to employ to protect its financial resources. The rationale is that the policies a borrowing member country follows in accordance with conditionality should enable it to terminate its use of Fund resources within a short period of time (Gold 1979).

There are good reasons why conditionality is attached to some forms of IMF financial assistance to member countries. One such derives from the

Table 2.2 *Selected financial activities of the IMF by type and country, 1976–83*

Activity	Financial year ended April 30								
	1976	1977	1978	1979	1980	1981	1982	1983	1976–83
I. General resources Account									
Gross purchases[a]	5,267.4	4,749.7	2,367.3	1,239.2	2,210.8	4,385.9	6,960.2	10,258.2	37,438.7
Net purchases[b]	(4,866.6)	(3,899.6)	(-1,861.8)	(-3,267.2)	(-1,041.8)	(-1,924.2)	(-4,950.3)	(-8,703.1)	(-18,173.0)
II. Administered accounts									
Trust funds loans	—	31.7	268.2	670.0	961.7	1,059.9	—	—	2,991.5
Oil facility subsidy account payments (grants)	13.8	27.5	25.0	19.1	27.8	50.1	9.3	2.5	175.1
Supplementary financing facility subsidy account payments (grants)	—	—	—	—	—	—	22.9	44.3	67.2
III. SDR allocations	—	—	—	4,032.6	4,033.2	4,052.5	—	—	12,118.3
Total	5,281.2	4,808.9	2,660.5	5,960.9	7,233.5	9,548.4	6,992.4	10,305.0	52,790.8
Industrial countries	2,391.3	2,198.1	1,438.8	2,593.7	2,617.6	2,543.9	—	54.0	13,837.5
Developing countries	2,889.9	2,610.8	1,221.7	3,367.2	4,615.9	7,004.3	6,992.4	10,250.0	38,953.3
Oil exporting	—	—	—	369.3	369.3	380.3	—	65.0	1,184.0
Non-oil developing	2,889.9	2,610.8	1,221.7	2,997.9	4,246.6	6,624.0	6,992.4	10,185.0	37,769.3
All countries	5,281.2	4,808.9	2,660.5	5,960.9	7,233.5	9,548.4	6,992.4	10,305.0	52,790.8

20

Memorandum: Stand-by and extended arrangements as of April 30

Commitments	1,472.2	5,197.6	5,759.3	1,600.4	3,049.7	9,475.1	16,206.3	25,025.5	—
As percentage of total quotas	5.0	17.8	17.8	4.1	7.8	15.9	26.7	41.0	—
Undrawn balances	1,085.8	3,581.1	3,638.8	1,377.5	2,718.0	8,076.4	11,154.6	16,405.1	—
As percentage of commitments	73.8	68.9	63.2	86.1	89.1	85.2	68.8	65.6	—
Gold distribution[c]	—	209.7	212.6	220.4	230.8	—	—	—	873.5
Profits from gold sales distributed to developing countries[d]	—	—	222.6	70.6	302.4	400.2	—	—	995.8

Figures in millions of SDRs.

[a]Excluding purchases in the reserve tranche.

[b]Excluding purchases and repurchases in the reserve tranche; net repurchases indicated by negative values.

[c]Valued at SDR 35 per fine ounce.

[d]Distribution in U.S. dollars. SDR amounts based on SDR/U.S. dollar rate in effect at time of distribution.

Source: IMF 1983.

traditional requirements of sound banking practice according to which lenders of funds generally ensure that borrowers are in a position to repay loans. Second, and as Article 1(V) indicates, adequate safeguards have to be taken to ensure the temporary and revolving character of loans. A third reason relates to the need for the IMF to exercise prudence in the rationing of its financial resources. As mentioned earlier, these resources are limited in relation to balance-of-payments adjustment needs of member countries. There is therefore an excess demand for the use of these resources, especially since IMF loans are available at rates of interest well below market rates (Bird 1979).

There are two types of conditionality: high and low. The conditionality attached to various IMF lending facilities is described in Table 2.3. High conditionality normally applies to the higher credit tranches, that is, the three credit tranches beyond the first credit tranche, including the supplementary financing facility and the extended financing facility. As the data in Table 2.4 show, the bulk of IMF lending since 1977 has been through purchases and under facilities that require high conditionality.

These high conditionality credits are typically provided under short-term stand-by arrangements, with an average repayment period of 12–18 months, but sometimes with extensions of up to three years. Borrowing under the stand-by arrangement guarantees the borrowing member an assured line of credit for a certain period of time. Drawings take the form of a series of installments, with their release dependent on the observance of certain "performance criteria." These performance criteria tend to be quite harsh and are based on both quantitative and qualitative indicators.

The quantitative performance criteria are usually implemented through agreements with borrowing member countries. In the typical case, the borrowing member must agree: (1) to eliminate budget deficits by reducing government expenditure, eliminating government subsidies, and/or by increasing taxes; and (2) to reduce government borrowing from the central bank, place ceilings on external borrowing, increase interest rates, and adjust the exchange rate (i.e., devalue the domestic currency). The qualitative criteria are designed to measure the extent to which the adjustment and stabilization programs are being satisfactorily implemented, and therefore whether IMF loans are being appropriately used. A qualitative criterion common to all stand-by agreements is that borrowing countries should avoid introducing exchange restrictions as a means of solving balance-of-payments problems.

IMF stabilization and adjustment programs are also based on certain "policy understandings." These are not the same as performance criteria, but rather are meant to reflect the overall policy environment in which stabilization and adjustment should take place. In general, the IMF would agree to provide short-term credit to a member country if the latter shows a willingness to pursue monetary, fiscal, and exchange-rate policies that are considered adequate to promote the desired quantitative targets.

Table 2.3 *Financial facilities of the Fund and their conditionality*

Reserve tranche
Condition—balance of payments need.

Tranche policies
First credit tranche
Program representing reasonable efforts to overcome balance-of-payments difficulties; performance criteria and installments not used.
Higher credit tranches
Transactions requiring that member give substantial justification of its efforts to overcome balance-of-payments difficulties; resources normally provided in the form of stand-by arrangements that include performance criteria and drawings in installments.

Extended Fund facility
Medium-term program for up to three years to overcome structural balance-of-payments maladjustments; detailed statement of policies and measures for first and subsequent 12-month periods; resources provided in the form of extended arrangements that include performance criteria and drawings in installments.

Compensatory financing facility
Existence of either a temporary export shortfall for reasons largely beyond the member's control or a temporary excess in the cost of cereal imports; member cooperates with Fund in an effort to find appropriate solutions for any balance-of-payments difficulties.

Buffer stock financing facility
Contribution to an international buffer stock accepted as suitable by Fund; member expected to cooperate with Fund as in the case of compensatory financing.

Enlarged access policy
For use in support of programs under stand-by arrangements reaching into the upper credit tranches or beyond, or under extended arrangements, subject to relevant policies on conditionality, phasing, and performance criteria.

Source: IMF 1982a.

These policy understandings normally cover the entire spectrum of policies related to the following areas, among others: (1) trade and exchange-rate policies designed to control excess absorption, provide export incentives, and to reduce the multiplicity of distortions in trade and exchange regimes; (2) interest rate and other pricing policies aimed at mobilizing domestic savings and improving resource allocation; (3) public sector policies concerning prices, taxes, and subsidies together with institutional reforms aimed at improving the efficiency of public sector activities, and

Table 2.4 *Low-conditionality and high-conditionality purchases, 1976–83*

Purchases	Financial year ended April 30							
	1976	1977	1978	1979	1980	1981	1982	1983
I. Low-conditionality purchases	5.09	2.97	0.41	0.64	1.05	1.56	1.65	4.12
First credit tranche	0.29	0.78	0.09	0.13	0.16	0.78	0.02	0.03
Oil facility	3.97	0.44	—	—	—	—	—	—
Compensatory financing facility	0.83	1.75	0.32	0.46	0.86	0.78	1.63	3.74
Buffer stock facility	—[a]	—	—	0.05	0.03	—	—	0.35
II. High-conditionality purchases	0.18	1.78	1.96	0.59	1.15	2.82	5.31	6.14
Credit tranche	0.17	1.59	1.85	0.35	0.93	1.90	2.73	3.68
Extended fund facility	0.01	0.19	0.11	0.24	0.22	0.92	2.58	2.46
III. Total I + II	5.27	4.75	2.37	1.23	2.20	4.38	6.96	10.26

Figures in billions of SDRs.
[a]Less than SDR 5 million.
Source: IMF 1983.

eliminating government budget deficits; and (4) income policies aimed at bringing claims on resources in line with their availability (Guitián 1981).

Once the policy understandings are reached based on appropriate domestic policies and the findings of an IMF mission to the country concerned, the member country usually "publishes" a "letter of intent" which sets out the objectives as well as the economic programs and policies it intends to pursue. If these are in line with the conditions required for drawing on the higher credit tranches, the borrowing member is then assured by a stand-by agreement that it will be able to purchase a specified amount of foreign exchange over the life of the agreement.

IMF stabilization programs are usually based on a close linkage between conditionality and the nature of the adjustment strategies which borrowing member countries are supposed to pursue. While such adjustment strategies may vary from case to case, the basic conditionality principle is one that stresses uniformity of treatment. The implication is that "for any given degree of need the effort of economic adjustment sought in programs be broadly equivalent among countries" (Guitián 1981, p. 2). On the other hand, the IMF also recognizes the need for flexibility, and that conditionality should take into account institutional characteristics and particular circumstances of countries. "In helping members to design adjustment programs, the Fund will pay due regard to the domestic social and political objectives, the economic priorities, and circumstances of members, including the causes of their balance of payments problems" (IMF 1979). However, while there is a recognition of the need to strike a delicate balance between uniformity of treatment and flexibility, the evidence suggests that, in the majority of cases, the uniformity principle is more closely adhered to. As a result, the IMF is usually criticized for what is perceived to be a "policy homogenization" across countries, irrespective of their individual economic circumstances.

We mentioned earlier that in the case of adjustment strategies designed to correct balance-of-payments disequilibria, the general interpretation is that such disequilibria reflect a situation in which the current account deficit is in excess of sustainable capital inflows from all potential sources. In this context, the determination of appropriate adjustment strategies is usually based on an assessment of the transience or permanence of the balance-of-payments disequilibria. Accordingly, a distinction is usually made between short-term payments disequilibria and more fundamental or structural ones associated with the long-term development process itself.

First, the short-term imbalances can take either of two forms. One type is considered to be temporary or cyclically reversible, in the sense that it is usually caused either by a temporary loss of markets and/or by a short-term deterioration in the terms of trade. When such a situation arises, very little or no change in policy is required. In the typical case, the payments deficit is financed either by short-term foreign loans and/or by drawing down of international reserves. IMF resources may also be used to build up the country's foreign reserve position. In any event, some IMF lending facilities (e.g., the buffer stock and compensatory financing mechanisms) can be used to cope with situations of this nature.

A second type of short-term imbalance may arise from a disequilibrium between aggregate demand and supply. This excess demand is usually traceable to monetary and fiscal policies that are considered to be too expansionary. In this case, the member countries concerned are expected to draw on the higher credit tranches of the Fund, and pursue the appropriate demand management policies. In this context, appropriate domestic fiscal and monetary policies are considered of critical importance in the attainment of a sustainable balance between aggregate demand and supply. (This aspect is taken up in greater detail in Chapter 3.) In some instances, the relevant monetary and fiscal (aggregate demand) policies are supported by debt management and income policies. This is a means of ensuring that, given a country's productive capacity and development prospects, total domestic resource demand will not exceed total potential supply.

The above types of disequilibria should be distinguished from the more fundamental disequilibria, which are a reflection of major structural weaknesses in the entire economy. This became particularly evident after the oil crises of the 1970s, when it was recognized that the imbalances that had developed in the international economy were not amenable to correction over a short period of time, and that the relevant adjustments would require substantial changes in the economies of IMF member countries. These factors have influenced IMF lending policies in the sense that the institution has become more willing to allow a relatively longer time frame for the adjustment effort, with an emphasis on more gradual changes in both aggregate demand and supply.

In this context, there has also been an increased recognition of the fact that aggregate demand management policies need to be complemented by others aimed at raising the level and/or rate of growth of aggregate supply, with the latter comprising resources which can be generated domestically plus those available from foreign sources. The reasoning is that aggregate supply is usually kept below its potential because of distortions in the structure of relative prices. Accordingly, the orthodox approach to this problem is predicated on the need for liberalization policies aimed at providing export incentives, and improving the overall allocation of resources.

The related policy measures are therefore concerned with correcting disparities between domestic and international prices as a means of restoring international competitiveness, redirecting resources to more productive sectors, and mobilizing domestic savings for needed investment purposes. The overall assumption is that the pursuit of such policies can prove instrumental in bringing the productive capacity of the economy back to its potential level and to a sustainable growth path, thereby lessening the degree of restraint called for in demand management and its supporting monetary and fiscal policies. Aspects of the liberalization ethic are further discussed in Part III.

The shift in the IMF's lending philosophy, which has accompanied changes in the nature of international adjustment problems, leads to the conclusion that it is no longer appropriate to make the conventional distinction between stabilization and adjustment, on the one hand, and development, on the other. The experience suggests that many adjustment problems are structural in nature, and therefore require a longer period for policies to show results. Policy measures designed to achieve a major reallocation of resources and to improve supply tend to alter the basic parameters of development, and the overall environment in which it takes place.

In a similar vein, an optimal mix of demand and supply management policies may be considered a necessary prerequisite for promoting economic development. While it may sometimes be difficult to distinguish demand and supply measures and their effects in practice, their complementarity can be looked at in terms of the two blades of Marshall's scissors. In this context, demand management provides an appropriate financial framework for growth and development in terms of the possibilities offered for mobilizing savings in relation to investment needs. However, its effectiveness from a development perspective depends on the extent to which it is complemented by supply-side measures, which are aimed at achieving a more efficient allocation of resources and the strengthening of the productive capacity of the economy.

This brings us to a consideration of IMF–World Bank policy symmetry, and the apparent convergence of their respective world views on development management, which seems to have happened in recent times. Agreement seems to have been reached over the recognition of a need for structural adjustment lending (as opposed to traditional forms of project lending), coupled with an increased emphasis on liberalization strategies. In the eyes of many, it has become increasingly difficult to distinguish the structural adjustment philosophy of the World Bank from the philosophy underlying the supply management policies of the IMF.

Whether or not one lends credence to this belief, it may be important to consider some of the factors at work. In the recent evolution of supply management and structural adjustment policies, a major watershed was provided by the World Bank's *World Development Report of 1981*, which examined the impact of inflation and recession in the industrial countries during the 1970s and rising oil prices on the adjustment process in developing countries (World Bank 1981a). The report emphasized the fact that most developing countries faced a difficult decade adjusting to changed external conditions, and therefore had to face the correspondingly difficult choice of reducing balance-of-payments deficits to sustainable levels.

Given the factors operating in the international environment, it was recognized that adjustment had to take place through shifts in international trade, changes in domestic production and consumption patterns, and through increased capital inflows. In the latter case, external borrowing was needed to accelerate investment and growth and to gain time for adjustment. However, it was also noted that countries that had borrowed heavily to support unsustainable patterns of production, consumption, and trade soon found themselves burdened with excessive debt and forced macroeconomic contraction.

One basic conclusion that emerged was that, given requisite changes in the international environment, countries should begin to pursue more outward-oriented development policies based on the alignment of their domestic prices with international prices. There was also the need for adjustment in three specific areas—trade, energy, and capital flows. To reiterate, it was in this context that the IMF shifted gears toward supply management, and the World Bank moved in the direction of structural adjustment lending. The policy symmetry that seems to have emerged between these two institutions is aptly captured in the following statement by the World Bank's senior vice-president:

> The Bank's structural adjustment lending clearly interfaces with the Fund's stabilization programs and extended facility arrangements. Both institutions now provide funds that are available to finance a broad range of imports, and both impose conditionality that requires the development of action programs focused on policy and management issues. The Fund is increasingly taking into account considerations of supply as well as demand management, and its programs now have a medium-term perspective. The Bank, for its part, is acutely aware that effective long-term development programs cannot be undertaken by a country that is disrupted by an immediate financial crisis. In such cases, priority must be given to stabilization measures. Experience over the past two years has shown that the Bank's SALs and the IMF programs are in practice both complementary and mutually reinforcing. (Stern 1983, p. 100)

Thus, in the policy approaches of both the World Bank and the IMF, it is now recognized that some countries may have to undertake programs of financial discipline (stabilization and demand management) as a means of moderating or reducing aggregate demand levels and bringing current account deficits to levels sustainable by external capital inflows. In both cases, emphasis is now being placed on policy and institutional reforms aimed at improving the efficiency of resource use.

In the latter context, a fundamental aim of structural adjustment lending is to strengthen the balance of payments over the medium and longer term through policies designed to improve economic efficiency. The associated policy measures are directed toward the restructuring of the incentives, improving the sectoral allocation of resources, revising public investment priorities, and strengthening institutions, especially in the public sector. An illustration is provided in Table 2.5.

Table 2.5   *The policy framework of structural adjustment lending*

Policy	Characteristic features
Trade	Exchange rate adjustment, export incentives, import liberalization, tariff reform, institutional support and development.
Production sectors	Energy: raise internal prices to encourage production and conservation; expand indigenous energy production capacity. Agriculture and industry: price incentives. Institutional reform: marketing, storage.
Public	Improving financial performance and efficiency of public enterprises and parastatals by restructuring priorities and strengthening institutional capacity to formulate and implement public investment programs. Improving resource allocation through more appropriate budgetary, expenditure, income, interest rate, and debt management policies; strengthening the institutional capacity to effect such policies.

Source: Compiled by author.

PART II

THE ECONOMICS OF ORTHODOX DEMAND MANAGEMENT

3

The Fundamentals of Macroeconomic Stabilization

The demand management focus of the IMF policy paradigm is based on an eclectic admixture of Keynesian and monetarist doctrines. This chapter highlights aspects of the approach that are in line with the Keynesian perspective of macroeconomic thinking. In this context, one basic assumption underlying the IMF approach is that balance-of-payments disequilibria facing developing countries are generally caused by an unsustainable expansion in aggregate demand relative to aggregate supply, and that this typically manifests itself in balance-of-payments deficits and inflation. The reasoning is that, at least in the short run, the level and rate of growth of aggregate supply are relatively stable, and therefore do not cause short-term fluctuations in output, prices, and the balance of payments.

The related policy thrust is therefore of an orthodox demand management variety. The general theory behind this policy can be explained as follows. In an open economy (i.e., one in which exchange rates are fixed, or at least where they are not totally flexible) if the rate of growth of aggregate demand exceeds the rate of growth of aggregate supply, the result will be domestic price increases and balance-of-payments deficits. When such a situation arises, the primary objective of demand management becomes one of restoring equilibrium between aggregate demand and aggregate supply, where the latter includes the value of domestic output plus net capital inflow from abroad. The restoration of macroeconomic equilibrium therefore involves either (1) the short-term stabilization or restructuring of domestic demand through the complementary use of monetary, fiscal, and exchange rate instruments, and/or (2) reducing domestic "absorption" in relation to income. The relevant analytical pillars supporting these two complementary approaches are further explained in the next two sections of the chapter.

THE SIMPLE ANALYTICS OF INCOME, ABSORPTION, AND BALANCE-OF-PAYMENTS INTERACTION

We begin by considering the principles underlying the need for reduced domestic absorption. In this case, the stabilization and restructuring of domestic demand involve the promotion of exports and import substitutes (what are termed "tradeables"), and a concomitant reduction of expenditures on "non-tradeables" or "home goods." This follows from assumptions about the relationship between national output, domestic absorption, and the balance of payments. The relationship is usually expressed in terms of the familiar Keynesian national income–expenditure identity, as follows:

$$Y = C + I + G + X - M \qquad\qquad 3.1$$

where Y is the national income, output, or aggregate demand; C is the private consumption expenditure; I is private investment; G is government expenditure of all kinds; X is exports of goods and services; and M is imports of goods and services.

Equation 3.1 can be interpreted to mean that national income or aggregate demand consists of goods and service produced domestically, exports, and the import content of private consumption, private investment, and government expenditure. From this, we may derive total absorption (TA), which consists of what is absorbed from domestic resources (AD) as well as from foreign sources, that is, imports (M). Thus,

$$TA = AD + M \qquad\qquad 3.2$$

with

$$AD = CD + ID + GD \qquad\qquad 3.3$$

or

$$AD = TA - M \qquad\qquad 3.4$$

D denotes "domestic."

The original national income or output Equation 3.1 can therefore be rewritten as:

$$Y = AD + X \qquad\qquad 3.5$$

or as

$$Y = TA - M + X \qquad\qquad 3.5a$$

or as

$$Y = TA + X - M \qquad \text{3.5b}$$

Alternatively, and in terms of total absorption,

$$Y - TA = X - M \qquad \text{3.6}$$

or

$$TA - Y = M - X \qquad \text{3.6a}$$

Equation 3.6a states that where there is a deficit in the current account of the balance of payments $(M - X)$, total absorption (TA) must exceed domestic output (Y) by the same amount. This depicts a situation in which a country is "living beyond its means," that is, it is spending or "absorbing" more than its domestic savings or income potential. When this happens, a foreign inflow of funds (foreign savings) is required to bring about a balance in the macroeconomy.

This macroeconomic balance is usually defined in terms of an equilibrium between savings (S) and investment (I). Therefore, the current account deficit $(M - X)$, or what is the same thing, the excess of total absorption over domestic output $(TA - Y)$, is really a reflection of the overall gap between investment and domestic savings $(I - S)$. This can be written as:

$$TA - Y = M - X = I - S \qquad \text{3.7}$$

Further, the savings–investment gap can be disaggregated into two components: a private component (P), and a public or government component (G). Thus

$$(I - S) = (IP - SP) + (IG - SG) \qquad \text{3.8}$$

The $(IG - SG)$ fraction on the right-hand side of the equation represents the government budget deficit, and is therefore a reflection of the extent of fiscal imbalance or disequilibrium. This element can therefore be written as

$$(IG - SG) = (G - T) \qquad \text{3.9}$$

The fraction $(G - T)$ defines the excess of government spending (G) over revenues (T). Equation 3.8 can therefore be reformulated as follows:

$$TA - Y = M - X = I - S = (IP - SP) + (G - T) \qquad \text{3.10}$$

In analytical terms, where the excess of absorption over domestic output $(TA - Y)$, or the current account deficit $(M - X)$ corresponds to the private savings–investment gap $(IP - SP)$, the imbalance can be rectified through an inflow of private capital. However, if the origin of the imbalance is considered to be the government budget deficit (excessive government spending, reflected in $G - T$), the proposed solution is a reduction in government spending (G), a raising of government revenues (T), and/or official capital inflows.

There are at least two general implications that follow from the above analysis. Where policy is directed toward reducing the government budget deficit, the implication is a reduction in domestic absorption, and/or an increase in domestic output. However, it is generally assumed in short-term stabilization programs that the latter course is not possible, so that the burden of adjustment must fall on aggregate demand management.

The other implication concerns the possibility of more private and official capital inflows as a means of financing the current account deficit. This aspect cannot be meaningfully discussed without considering the overall balance-of-payments position, and, in particular, the capital account. These and other related considerations are taken up below.

FISCAL–MONETARY DISEQUILIBRIUM AND BUDGET DEFICIT FINANCING

As indicated earlier, a fundamental assumption underlying orthodox demand management and stabilization programs is that the expansion of aggregate demand and related balance-of-payments deficits stems mainly from inappropriate fiscal and monetary policies. These are, in turn, reflected in fiscal and monetary imbalances. The fiscal disequilibria are assumed to arise from levels of government expenditure that exceed the capacity to raise revenues. This is in turn linked to a monetary disequilibrium, on the assumption that the government has to borrow in order to finance its budget deficit, thereby causing strains on the domestic banking sector. The related policy prescriptions emphasize the use of a combination of monetary and fiscal measures as a means of achieving a sustainable rate of aggregate demand and a viable balance-of-payments position.

The management of fiscal policy, as alluded to earlier, usually involves measures to restrain government spending and/or to raise government revenues in order to effect an equilibrium between the public sector budget and the amount of financing available. In terms of the linkage with monetary policy, the goal is usually to restrict the expansion of domestic credit, and therefore the money supply, to levels consistent with the reduction of the inflation rate to a certain target level. Restrictions are therefore placed on the expansion of net domestic assets and borrowing by the government from the central bank. Some of the assumptions commonly made about the behavior of monetary and fiscal variables and their relationship to the overall balance of payments may now be highlighted. The exposition draws on Khan and Knight (1981), Crockett (1981), and Dornbusch (1980).

A convenient starting point is a consideration of how the budget deficit is financed, as well as the implications for the overall balance of payments. First, the government fiscal deficit $(G - T)$ is usually financed through a combination of three mechanisms: (1) credit extended by the domestic banking system, and mainly from the central bank; (2) borrowing domestically from the private non-bank sector; and/or (3) foreign loans. An equation for government deficit financing can therefore be written as

$$(G - T) = (\Delta DCG + \Delta DCPLG + \Delta FKG) \qquad 3.11$$

where ΔDCG is the net claims of the banking system on the government; $\Delta DCPLG$ is the net claims of the domestic non-bank sector on the government; ΔFKG is foreign loans; and Δ is the change from one time period to another.

In most developing countries, however, borrowing from the domestic non-bank sector is negligible, because of the relatively undeveloped nature of financial and capital markets. This aspect of financing is therefore not given any further consideration. As a result, Equation 3.11 can be written as

$$(G - T) = (\Delta DCG + \Delta FKG) \qquad 3.12$$

Equation 3.12 emphasizes the two primary sources of financing, domestic and foreign. In other words, the government's overall budget balance or deficit can be subdivided into both domestic and foreign components, with total expenditures and revenues treated in a similar manner. Thus

$$G = GD + GF \qquad 3.13$$

and

$$T = TD + TF \qquad 3.14$$

where D and F represent domestic and foreign, respectively.

Using Equations 3.12 through 3.14, the budget deficit can be expressed as

$$(G - T) = GD + GF - TD - TF \qquad 3.15$$

or as

$$(G - T) = (GD - TD) + (GF - TF) \qquad\qquad 3.15a$$

where $(GD - TD)$ is the domestic deficit and $(GF - TF)$ is the foreign deficit.

In terms of financing, and using Equation 3.12, we obtain

$$(GD - TD) + (GF - TF) = \Delta DCG + \Delta FKG \qquad\qquad 3.16$$

or

$$(GD - TD) = (\Delta DCG + \Delta FKG) - (GF - TF) \qquad\qquad 3.16a$$

All the terms on the right-hand side of the equation represent elements of domestic liquidity. The budget deficit therefore has a direct effect on the creation of domestic liquidity, that is, the money supply process. Some wider implications for money creation and the overall balance of payments are explained below.

First, in order to show the impact of total money creation, we introduce an equation showing how the private sector budget balance or deficit is financed. The reasoning is similar to that used for the public sector. In other words, any private sector savings–investment gap ($IP - SP$ in Equation 3.8) is financed through a combination of domestic credit and foreign capital inflows, but mainly in the form of direct foreign investment. Analogously, these two basic forms of financing can be illustrated as follows:

$$(IP - SP) = \Delta DCP + \Delta FKP \qquad\qquad 3.17$$

where ΔDCP is domestic credit to the private sector and ΔFKP is foreign finance of the private sector.

Alternatively, and as was done for the public sector, the private sector savings–investment equation can be disaggregated into its domestic and foreign components, as follows:

$$(IPD - SPD) = (\Delta DCP + \Delta FKP) - IPF - SPF \qquad\qquad 3.18$$

Equation 3.18 is the private sector equivalent of the public sector equation, 3.16a. In a similar way, the right-hand side of Equation 3.18 shows the direct effect on liquidity creation that results from the private domestic savings–investment gap.

The monetary or liquidity implications of the overall macroeconomic disequilibrium or "overabsorption" can now be expressed by combining Equations 3.11, 3.12, and 3.17. Therefore,

$$(IP - SP) + (G - T) = \Delta DCP + \Delta DCG + \Delta FKP + \Delta FKG \qquad 3.19$$

The above equation links the overall macroeconomic picture, suitably disaggregated into its private and public sector components, to the overall availability of liquidity. One element of the latter is represented by changes in the banking system's claims on the private sector (ΔDCP) combined with similar claims on the government (ΔDCG). The other element reflects the availability of foreign sources of liquidity, either in the form of direct foreign investment in the private sector (ΔFKP) and/or loans to the public sector (ΔFKG). Stated differently, the banking system's claims on the combined private and public sectors represent changes in total domestic credit (ΔDC), while the foreign borrowing by the private and government sectors, as well as any foreign balances that might have accumulated in the past, will be reflected in the net foreign asset position of the economy. This is depicted by the fraction (ΔNFA) in Equation 3.20 below.

$$(IP - SP) + (G - T) = \Delta DC + \Delta NFA \qquad 3.20$$

This is a simplified form of Equation 3.19. The right-hand side of the equation represents the total liquidity creation in the economy, or all forms of money and quasi-money. Thus

$$(IP - SP) + (G - T) = \Delta DC + \Delta NFA = \Delta M \qquad 3.21$$

where (ΔM) represents changes in the money supply.

Equation 3.21 provides some indication of how the balance-of-payments deficit is financed. Reintroducing the expression for the current account deficit ($M - X$) from Equation 3.11, the following equation can be derived:

$$(IP - SP) + (G - T) = (I - S) = (M - X)$$

$$= (\Delta DC + \Delta NFA) - \Delta M \qquad 3.22$$

The equation implies that the current account deficit or the macroeconomic disequilibrium between savings and investment can take place through: (1) increases in domestic credit (ΔDC), (2) changes in net foreign assets (ΔNFA), reflecting a combination of private and official foreign borrowing and changes in external reserves; and (3) any offsetting changes in the money supply (ΔM).

In the context of IMF stabilization and adjustment (demand management) programs, therefore, the avoidance of macroeconomic and balance-of-payments disequilibria requires that domestic credit creation should be kept in line with the growth of domestic liquidity. Adherence to this rule is considered important if the inflation rate is to be kept within sustainable bounds. In terms of the policy-analytic approach the IMF actually follows, when payments and macroeconomic disequilibria occur in member countries, it is first ascertained whether any additional external finance is available (i.e., in terms of ΔNFA). Second, an attempt is made to predict the demand for domestic liquidity (ΔM), based on assumptions about inflation and the economy's real growth rate. These parameters are then used to determine the residual expansion of domestic credit that will be allowed.

It is at this stage that the IMF's demand management or "financial programming" package comes into play. As indicated earlier, it typically involves the imposition of ceilings on domestic credit and external borrowing, in order to ensure that there are no excessive loans to the government to finance its budget deficit and, in general, that there are no forms of finance that are judged to be out of line with the requirements of the balance-of-payments adjustment process. These requirements are normally set out in terms of specific balance-of-payments targets to be achieved in the future. The policy–theoretical framework is also heavily influenced by the IMF's own model of the "Monetary Approach to the Balance of Payments," to which some reference is made in Chapter 5 below.

UNDERSTANDING THE MONEY SUPPLY PROCESS

In order to lend completeness to the foregoing analysis, some attention must be paid to factors underlying the money supply process. It is evident that the practice of sound demand management requires an understanding of its behavior, as well as how it can be controlled in the pursuit of macroeconomic objectives. In this context, a convenient point of departure lies in considering the concept of the money stock. Money stock is an outgrowth of the behavior of the government or public sector (primarily through the Ministry of Finance), the Central Bank, the private financial sector (including commercial banks and other financial intermediaries), as well as from actions emanating from the rest of the world.

The money stock (M) can be defined as a multiple (m) of what is usually termed the *money base* (B), with the latter representing liabilities of the central bank. The relationship is shown in Equation 3.23:

$$M = mB \qquad\qquad 3.23$$

where M is the narrow stock of money; B is the money base (all forms of money and quasi-money); and m is the money multiplier. As can be gleaned from Equation 3.23, the money stock is usually larger than the money base. This is as a result of the fractional reserve system that has traditionally defined banking arrangements in the Western world. In this system, financial institutions have been able to create lending capacities which are a multiple of the deposits made with them. It is in this context that the money multiplier comes into play. It does not purport to explain the behavior of the money stock per se, but rather what is likely to happen to this stock if the supply or sources of, and the demand or uses for, the money stock are in equilibrium. The money multiplier is therefore a useful concept in furthering our understanding of the complex sets of interrelationships that are usually involved in the money supply process.

The nature of the interactive processes can be viewed in terms of the sources from which the money base is derived:

$$B = DCG + NFA + DCB + OA \qquad\qquad 3.24$$

where DCG is the central bank credit to the government (as before); NFA is the net foreign assets of the central bank (as before); DCB is the central bank credit to commercial banks; and OA is miscellaneous assets.

As indicated earlier, the borrowing needs of the government are usually met through the provision of credit by the central bank. One assumption that is usually made in IMF stabilization programs, and which is borne out by the facts, is that the government's borrowing needs, as usually expressed through demands made by the Ministry of Finance, tend to dominate the money base (i.e., through DCG), and this forms the primary mechanism through which the budget deficit is financed.

An extremely small proportion of the government debt in developing countries is privately held, but to the extent that this occurs, changes in DCG, and therefore in the money base, are likely to take place through the effects of open market operations. The net foreign assets component of the money base (i.e., NFA) is related to external dealings and basically reflects changes in the structure of trade and international capital movements. Central bank credit to commercial banks reflects reserves borrowed from the central bank, and these can be controlled directly or indirectly through the central bank's discount rate (the rate charged for borrowed reserves).

Following from the above, and given the relatively unsophisticated banking systems existing in most developing countries, the money stock can be defined in terms of the public's holdings of currency and demand deposits. In this context, the money base reflects the public's demand for currency as well as the demand for reserves by the commercial banks. The equation for the money stock can therefore be expressed as follows:

$$M = DMD + CURR \qquad\qquad 3.25$$

and

$$B = RES + CURR \qquad\qquad 3.26$$

Where *DMD* is demand deposits; *CURR* is currency in circulation; and *RES* is required bank reserves. Further, the following three additional conditions can be presumed to hold:

$$RES = r_1 (DMD + SVD) \qquad\qquad 3.27$$

$$CURR = r_2 (DMD) \qquad\qquad 3.28$$

$$SVD = r_3 (DMD) \qquad\qquad 3.29$$

where *SVD* is savings or time deposits.

The r_1 ratio depends on the reserve requirements for deposits in the commercial banks. For developed economies, a distinction is sometimes made between "required" and "excess" reserves. However, this distinction does not have much significance for a typical developing country where it can be assumed that commercial banks will expand their loans to the maximum level permitted by their reserve assets. The r_2 ratio depends on the public's preference for money in the form of cash in checking acounts. This preference, in turn, is determined by factors such as income levels, the distribution of income, interest rates, and the extent of financial development. The r_3 ratio depends on the structure of interest rates in both official and unorganized financial markets.

In simple algebraic terms, the equations for both the money base and the money stock can be reinterpreted by manipulating Equations 3.25 through 3.29. First, by substituting Equations 3.27 and 3.28 into Equation 3.26, we obtain

$$B = r_1 (DMD + SVD) + r_2 (DMD) \qquad\qquad 3.30$$

Second, substituting Equation 3.29 into 3.30 yields

$$B = (r_1 + r_2 + r_3) DMD \qquad\qquad 3.31$$

or

$$DMD = \frac{1}{(r_1 + r_2 + r_3)} B \qquad\qquad 3.31a$$

Using Equation 3.31a, currency can be defined in terms of the money base, as follows:

$$CURR = \frac{r_2}{(r_1 + r_2 + r_3)} B \qquad\qquad 3.32$$

Substituting Equations 3.25, 3.31a, and 3.32 yields

$$M = \frac{(1 + r_2)}{(r_1 + r_2 + r_3)} B \equiv mB \qquad\qquad 3.33$$

or

$$M = \frac{(1 + r_2)}{(r_1 + r_2 + r_3)} (DCG + NFA + DCB + OA) \equiv mB \qquad 3.34$$

Equations 3.33 and 3.34 describe equilibrium conditions for the money stock, or what is sometimes called the *money supply function.* They also highlight the influence of the money multiplier. This influence operates through a relationship between the money base, the public's demand for currency, and the reserves of commercial banks. A more extensive discussion of these relationships can be found in the excellent volume by Coats and Khatkhate (1980).

One policy conclusion that forms the basis of IMF demand management and stabilization programs is that the central bank is able to exert control over the money supply. This view draws support from the monetarist perspective which posits that the variables entering the money supply function are relatively stable and predictable, and therefore can be controlled by the monetary authorities. As an example, it is thought that the behavior of the money multiplier can be predicted within reasonable bounds, based on estimates of the behavior of currency, bank reserves, and the money base. This base is in turn influenced by the nature of government budget deficits and balance-of-payments profiles.

There is empirical evidence which suggests that the behavior of the money multiplier in most developing countries is relatively stable, and that the behavior of the money supply is dominated by the money base over relatively long periods of time. However, this conclusion must be tempered by the fact that both the money multiplier and the nature of the interactive processes ultimately depend on the definition of money that is used. As indicated in the next chapter, this poses a difficult problem in most developing countries, because of the relatively underdeveloped nature of their financial systems.

4

Financial Growth and
The Development Process

Monetary orthodoxy posits that most of the variables entering the supply function for money are stable and predictable, but to the extent that some of them cannot be controlled by the monetary authorities, certain policy instruments can be used to offset any independent influences on the money supply. The validity of the approach depends on the efficiency with which the financial system functions and its level of institutional development. This chapter outlines some characteristic features of financial systems in developing countries, as well as some requirements for their future development.

UNDERDEVELOPED FINANCIAL SYSTEMS: SOME STYLIZED FACTS

While the structure and degree of sophistication of financial systems vary considerably among developing countries, some basic characteristics are common to most of them. In general, they are relatively underdeveloped, oligopolistic, and replete with a large number of market imperfections and externalities. These conditions, in turn, tend to militate against their efficient functioning.

First, government-owned financial institutions usually play a major role in these systems, even when large foreign-owned institutions are present. The government's influence is usually linked to some other characteristic features, including: (1) the fact that the central bank is the primary source of funds to the economy; (2) irrespective of the nature of the political system, the public sector tends to be the major borrower of funds from the financial system; and (3) government-owned banks and other financial institutions are usually the major suppliers of funds to parastatals and other non-financial institutions.

Second, the financial system tends to be relatively unsophisticated, and is segmented into a limited number of financial institutions. In the typical case, it comprises a handful of deposit money banks, a few specialized banks, one or two development banks, and a few small savings institutions including credit unions, provident societies, and a postal checking and savings account system.

Third, the activities of traditional moneylenders usually form an important complement to those of organized financial markets. The moneylenders play an important role in the process of financial intermediation by providing financial services to rural areas, as well as to that part of the urban population without access to the organized portion of the financial system. These segments of the population form part of what is thought of as an "informal" market in which interest rates are substantially higher than the maximum lending rates allowed on loans in the organized financial sector. Institutions in the official or organized financial sector typically find it unprofitable to make loans to the segments of the population mentioned above because of the high administrative costs and the risks associated with handling relatively small-sized loans.

Fourth, the most important interest rates in most developing countries are determined by administrative fiat, and typically through legally imposed rates charged for bank lending and savings deposits. In passing, it should be mentioned that many governments have felt it necessary to maintain control over these rates in order to ensure that a few large financial institutions do not dominate the financial market, as well as to offset any possible distortions on investment, prices, production, and foreign trade. One systematic effect is that the official or organized financial sector in many developing countries is now defined by low nominal, and at times, negative real interest rates (i.e., nominal interest rates corrected for inflation). As the data in Table 4.1 show, these interest rates are often negative by a substantial margin.

Where interest rates in official markets are either low or negative, a substantial amount of funds is usually diverted away into the black or parallel market. Another systematic effect is for people to hold a large proportion of their wealth and savings in inflationary hedges such as real estate, consumer durables, art, and foreign currency holdings, rather than in domestic assets. The overall result is an upward pressure on prices, a weakening of the home currency position in foreign exchange markets, and a reduction in the amount of financial savings available for investment.

Fifth, the financial mobilization and intermediation processes in many developing countries have been consistently thwarted by certain "barriers to entry" imposed through both the public and private decision-making process. The underlying factors include: (1) the lack of confidence between surplus monetary units, or net savers/lenders, on the one hand, and their deficit counterparts, or net borrowers, on the other; (2) uncertainties

Table 4.1 *Rates of interest and inflation in selected developing countries*

Country	Rate of[a] interest	Percentage change in consumer price index	Interest rate adjusted for inflation[b]		
	July 1980	July 1980– June 1981	July 1980– June 1981	July 1979– June 1980	July 1978– June 1979
Argentina[c]	107.8	94.3	6.9	-3.8	-17.1
Brazil[d]	73.2	106.3	-16.0	-13.1	-0.4
Chile[c]	37.9	21.0	14.0	13.1	18.2
Ghana	13.0	118.2	-48.2	-19.6	-36.4
Greece	16.0	23.3	-5.9	-11.8	-3.6
India	7.0	13.7	-5.9	-4.4	0.5
Indonesia	9.0	9.0	0.0	-7.9	-12.4
Ivory Coast	7.2	2.5	4.6	-8.3	-10.2
Jamaica	9.0	11.5	2.2	-15.9	-15.1
Kenya	6.3	11.8	-4.9	-7.1	-1.7
Korea	23.0	25.6	-1.3	-6.2	-0.8
Malaysia	7.0	11.2	-3.1	-0.1	3.7
Mexico[e]	15.6	27.8	-9.5	-8.7	-2.4
Pakistan	12.0	15.0	-2.6	0.7	2.5
Portugal	21.0	17.6	2.9	3.7	-2.6
Turkey	33.0	28.9	3.2	-47.0	-28.3
Venezuela	12.0	17.7	-4.8	-8.8	-2.2

[a]Unless otherwise indicated the rate on one-year time deposits.

[b]Computed as $100[(1 + i)/(1 + p) - 1]$ where i is the nominal interest rate, p is the percentage change in the consumer price index, and both are expressed in decimal form.

[c]The interest rate is the yield on one-month time deposits compounded over the relevant 12-month period. Longer-term rates are unimportant because of the dominance of the shorter term.

[d]The interest rate is the annualized yield on two-year treasury bonds, including interest and monetary correction.

[e]Data, for July 1980 to June 1981 only, taken from *International Reports Statistical Market Letter,* various issues.

Source: Lanyi and Saracoglu (1983).

about the behavior of the economy; (3) the fear of disclosure of wealth, since this may invite taxation or other redistributive measures; (4) the smallness of domestic markets, and the lumpiness of investment requirements; (5) the concentration of wealth, and therefore potential savings, in a few hands; and (6) the channelling of potential savings into conspicuous forms of consumption (Reynolds 1969).

Some analysts (Shaw 1973; McKinnon 1973) have also emphasized the pervasiveness of "financial repression" or the absence of "financial deepening" in the financial systems of developing countries. Evidence of financial repression or shallowness is traceable to the existence of the following conditions, among others: the fragmentation of financial and output markets; the nonspecialization of financial functions by financial intermediaries; the oligopolistic or high-cost structure of the banking system; the heavy reliance on fiscal policy; and the flight of domestic capital abroad. By contrast, financial development is usually accompanied by financial deepening, which is defined by an expansion and differentiation of the financial superstructure, an increase in domestic liquidity, and a growth in foreign reserves induced through the use of more appropriate domestic pricing policies.

SAVINGS, ACCUMULATION, AND THE FINANCIAL INTERMEDIATION PROCESS

This brings us to a consideration of some of the linkages that are commonly perceived to exist between the growth of monetary and financial institutions and the wider development process. In this context, a general hypothesis is that, as development proceeds, mechanisms have to be created for channelling the surplus funds of savers toward investors whose demand for such funds tends to exceed their own savings. The reasoning is that this dichotomous relationship between savers and investors, and the related disequilibrium between savings and investment, can be increasingly bridged through the creation of various financial liabilities. These, in turn, represent indirect claims, via financial institutions, which channel the surplus funds of savers to those individuals who desire them for real capital investment (Coats and Khatkhate 1980).

In this context, financial intermediaries become the major channels for mobilizing and redeploying savings. The financial surpluses and savings of the economy can be mobilized in several alternative ways, including, among other things: self-financing, foreign borrowing, fiscal means, inflationary finance, and through debt-asset or intermediation techniques. Therefore, the general consensus is that financial intermediation tends to take on added significance as financial markets become more sophisticated, and as developing countries intensify their efforts to raise their own domestic savings rates.

However, there is no consensus about the specific type of financial intermediation required for development, or the direction of causation. What is generally agreed on is that some form of financial intermediation is required, and that its level of sophistication tends to be positively correlated with levels and rates of growth of savings, investment, and the overall development process. As indicated earlier, one underlying argument is that development tends to be associated with an increasing distinction between surplus and deficit saving units. Further, according to Gurley and Shaw (1964), there seems to be an inevitability about this dichotomous situation that is related to changes in both the structure of production and the distribution of income and wealth which accompany economic growth.

In the view of such analysts, the process involves at least three interdependent forms of division of labor in economic activity: (1) changes in production, involving factor services and inputs; (2) accumulation and savings; and (3) intermediation. The reasoning is that, as the economy develops, there is an associated differentiation in productive activities and specialization in productive functions. Changes in the structure and function take place at different points in space and time, so that some economic units would have greater access to financial resources than others. Surplus units would save those funds that remain after internal requirements for consumption and investment are met. Intermediation comes into play as a mechanism for transforming savings into new investment, thereby providing impetus to the cumulative cycle of economic activity.

Finally, a few brief remarks should be addressed to the perceived relationships between capital accumulation, savings, and financial intermediation. A convenient point of departure is the well-known Harrod-Domar growth model which postulates that capital accumulation not only creates capital capacity, but also generates output, income, and employment. In the model, the entire growth in output or income is attributed to investment or the past growth of capital, with the relationship between output growth and investment represented by the capital/output ratio. The model represents the relationship as a purely technological one, with the rate of growth of output determined by the proportion of past output that has been used for capital formation. The resulting generalization is that the main obstacle to the development of relatively poor countries lies in the pervasive lack of capital formation to meet their required investment needs.

The relationship between capital capacity creation and economic growth can be explained in the following terms. If we assume a constant ratio of savings to income (s) and a constant capital-to-output ratio (k), output and incomes will be increased by $(s/k)Y$, where Y equals national income or output, s the average propensity to save, and k the capital-to-output ratio. The increase in income or output therefore depends on the increase in capital capacity, as follows:

$$\Delta Y = \frac{s}{k} \ Y \qquad\qquad\qquad 4.1$$

and

$$\frac{\Delta Y}{Y} = \frac{s}{k} \qquad\qquad\qquad 4.2$$

where

$$s = \frac{S}{Y} = \frac{\Delta S/Y}{\Delta Y/Y} \qquad\qquad 4.3$$

and

$$k = \frac{K}{Y} = \frac{\Delta K/Y}{\Delta Y/Y} \qquad\qquad 4.4$$

where S is the total savings and K is the total capital stock.

Using the schema developed by Wai (1972), the relationship between the savings ratio, investment, and financial intermediation can now be stated as follows:

$$\frac{S}{Y} = \frac{S}{\Delta F} \times \frac{\Delta F}{I} \times \frac{I}{Y} \qquad\qquad 4.5$$

where S/Y is the ratio of national savings to GNP; $S/\Delta F$ is the financial intermediation multiplier; $\Delta F/I$ is the proportion of domestic investment financed through the intermediation process; and I/Y is the investment rate.

Equation 4.5 states that the national savings rate (S/Y) depends on the interplay of three sets of factors: (1) the financial intermediation multiplier $(S/\Delta F)$; (2) the proportion of domestic investment financed by savings mobilized and redeployed through the intermediation process $(\Delta F/I)$; and (3) the investment rate (I/Y).

Underlying the investment coefficient is the assumption that the achievement of any desired rate of growth requires a certain rate of capital formation or investment expenditure. As stated earlier, the investment rate depends on the interaction between the overall rate of growth of the economy and the incremental capital-to-output ratio. This relationship can be expressed as follows:

$$\frac{I}{Y} = \frac{\Delta K}{\Delta Y} \times \frac{\Delta Y}{Y} \qquad\qquad 4.6$$

where $\Delta K/\Delta Y$ is the incremental capital-to-output ratio; and $\Delta Y/Y$ is the national income or output growth rate.

The higher the investment rate, the greater will be the amount of surplus funds left over after consumption and reinvestment requirements are met. The extent to which these funds are rechannelled to deficit spending units (i.e., borrowers) ultimately depends on the efficiency of the financial intermediation process. As shown in Equation 4.5, the investment rate is closely related to the national savings rate, and must be matched by a corresponding savings ratio in order to assure macroeconomic balance. At a more disaggregated level, the interaction between the investment ratio and national income or output depends on the nature of the interaction that takes place with private and government savings.

While orthodox theorists generally agree about the pivotal role of capital accumulation in the growth process, they provide different interpretations of what is perceived to be the relatively low rates of capital accumulation in the developing countries. Some identify the incentive to save as the critical factor. For example, Nurske (1953) explains the nature of investment incentives in terms of the concept of the vicious circle, implying that there is a circular constellation of forces which tend to keep developing countries in a state of poverty.

While some theorists identify the incentive to invest as limiting the rate of investment in reproducible capital, others see the capacity to save as posing the main obstacle. In general, this perspective stresses the inability of poor masses to save, due to insufficient margins above subsistence income. It is also argued that the consumption habits prevalent in developing countries are such that the available surplus tends to be used up in conspicuous consumption as a direct result of the demonstration effect of the consumption habits in the developed societies. This low level of savings, when invested, proves insufficient in terms of maintaining per capita output.

One strategy, suggested by Lewis (1954, 1955), is to increase the capacity to save of those who can save. This implies an encouragement of savings by the capitalist class whose members are considered the primary savers in the economy. Accordingly, the distribution of income should be shifted to favor the savings/capitalist class whose members are the profit earners, with the largest incomes in society, and constituting about 10 percent of the population. According to Lewis, the growth of the capitalist class (people who think in terms of investing capital productively) constitutes a necessary condition for development. By contrast, the growth of the noncapitalist class (in the form of more income to noncapitalists is not considered to be conducive to capital accumulation, and therefore growth.

Finally, while theorists of all persuasions would agree that the capital factor plays an important role in the development process, there still remains no consensus about its overall importance. One problem is related to the fact that it is difficult to measure capital, so that the use of the capital-to-output ratio as a tool in development planning becomes highly questionable. It is also questionable whether the rate of savings and capital accumulation in many developing countries is in fact low, and whether this is a major cause of their poor economic performance.

In the latter context, empirical evidence suggests that the average gross domestic savings are more or less the same for low-, middle-, and higher-income countries: 23, 25, and 22 percent, respectively, during the late 1970s (World Bank 1981). The evidence also indicates a range of savings as wide as 2 to 32 percent within low- and middle-income countries, and 11 to 42 percent within the high-income countries. There are countries at low per capita income levels with relatively high savings rates, while there are many high-income countries with relatively low savings rates.

The evidence also suggests that in many developing countries the savings and capital accumulation process has taken a form different from that which is common to the developed Western world. For example, asset accumulation in the form of temples, pyramids, and related artifacts, while not directly productive, do represent meaningful dimensions of savings and accumulation. What this suggests is that a meaningful assessment of capital's role must take into account the requisite system of cultural values. Further, while the level of institutional savings may be low in some developing countries, it seems quite rational for large numbers of people to hold their savings in readily redeemable non-market instruments such as gold and jewelry.

Another set of considerations relates to the distinction conventionally made between investment and savings on the hand, and consumption, on the other. In a development context, consumption should be considered complementary to, rather than in competition with, investment. The reference here is to average consumption levels rather than to the highly conspicuous consumption of high-income groups. Where people are already at very low consumption levels, the provision of certain consumer goods may very well serve as an inducement to greater economic effort and performance. This is also true of expenditures on items such as nutrition, education, and the provision of related basic social services. Not only do such expenditures help to improve the ability to work, and therefore productivity, but they are also developmental in terms of their contribution to the fulfillment of basic human needs. In other words, output expansion and overall development may take place by *investing in people,* with a reduced emphasis on investment in physical capital. (An extensive and penetrative discussion along these lines can be found in Streeten 1981, 1982.)

5
Monetarist Perspectives

The focus now shifts to certain aspects of monetarist thought, as a means of highlighting another theoretical pillar that is synergistic with the IMF policy paradigm. It should be stated at the outset that there are several versions of monetarist economics. This is also the case for Keynesian economics. Economists who label themselves "monetarists" sometimes have internal disagreements which are as sharp as any among those who call themselves "Keynesians." However, from the perspective of orthodox demand management, the most influential variety of monetarism continues to be that associated with University of Chicago macroeconomics.

SOME BASIC PROPOSITIONS OF MONETARISM

A convenient starting point is the well-known quantity theory of money, and Milton Friedman's restatement of this doctrine (Friedman 1956). It is based on the idea that changes in the stock of money are the primary determinants of total spending, and therefore the overall level of economic activity. This can be contrasted with non-monetarist, especially Keynesian approaches, which do not place so much emphasis on monetary impulses. The latter approaches, while agreeing that money matters to some extent, place emphasis on both monetary and fiscal instruments, and argue that other components of aggregate demand tend to have a significant impact on economic activity.

A second central tenet of monetarism is that a stable demand function for money exists, and that this demand function provides the logical link between the monetary and real sectors of the economy. According to Friedman: "The quantity theory is in the first instance a theory of the demand for money . . . and the theory of the demand for money is a special topic in the theory of capital" (1956, p. 4). This implies that money is an asset or capital good that yields income, with capital being the present value of income. Friedman bases his analysis on a broad concept of wealth that encompasses all human and non-human sources of income. He relates the demand for money to total wealth and the expected future streams of money income that can be obtained from holding wealth in alternative forms.

A third proposition emphasizes the close relationship between nominal money and the price level. In general, monetarists, following the quantity theory approach, argue that an increase in money tends to have a direct effect on expenditures, prices, and a wide variety of implicit yields on assets. In this regard, a fundamental proposition is that movements in the quantity of money tend to provide the most reliable measure of monetary impulses, and that these are transmitted to the real sector of the economy via relative prices.

The view essentially postulates that, in the long run, growth of output and employment are determined by society's resources. The price level is simply the rate at which money can be exchanged for this output. Since the behavior of prices over time is determined by the growth in the money stock relative to the growth of output, total spending and the rate of inflation are uniquely dependent on the money supply.

One implication of the theory, therefore, is that any sustained increase in the rate of growth of the money supply tends to generate inflation and inflationary expectations. Under such circumstances, if an attempt is made to slow inflation by reducing the rate of money growth, output and employment will be temporarily reduced, but high wages and prices will persist due to inflationary expectations. Therefore, the spending response will lead to a contraction of output and employment, but not to an immediate fall in the price level. This leads to a possibility of inflation and higher levels of unemployment coexisting for some time.

This possibility arises because monetary policy "cannot peg the rate of unemployment for more than limited periods" (Friedman 1969, p. 99). As is well known to economists, this is another way of stating the hypothesis of the "natural rate of unemployment," that unemployment in the long run will settle at its "natural rate," irrespective of the rate of inflation. The logic behind this approach is that the Phillips curve tradeoff between inflation and unemployment will tend to disappear as soon as workers' expectations adapt to the actual inflation rate and incorporate the fully anticipated inflation rate into their wage bargains.

One implication of this model is that unemployment is a voluntary phenomenon, in the sense that it constitutes the free choice of those who are unemployed. If those who are "naturally unemployed" are willing to change occupations, areas of residence, or work for lower wages, they will be able to find work. It also suggests that policy should be non-interventionist.

Another implication is that policy designed to increase output in the short run, by increasing the growth in the money supply, will result in inflation. On the other hand, the attempt to slow inflation by reducing the money supply growth rate will result in unemployment, but with no abatement in the rate of inflation. The related policy conclusion is that the use of monetary policy as a short-term stabilization tool may prove costly in terms of unfavorable price movements, as well as in terms of losses in output and employment. However, it is argued that these costs will be minimized if monetary policy is used as a long-term stabilization tool.

A fundamental policy implication of monetarist thought, therefore, is that there should be a steady and moderate growth rate in the money supply, if inflation and inflationary expectations are to be curbed. It is in this context that regulation of the money base becomes the primary instrument through which the money stock is controlled. One by-product of this perspective is that fiscal policy does not matter, and unless it is accompanied by an accommodating monetary policy, it would prove powerless in terms of influencing output and the price level. A related hypothesis is that government spending, especially when financed by taxing or borrowing from the public, tends to "crowd out" private spending.

EXTENSIONS TO THE OPEN ECONOMY

Elements of the monetarist approach have been incorporated into several macroeconomic models of the open economy and the international adjustment process. The most well known is what is termed "the monetary approach to the balance of payments," which studies the interaction between money and external payments. There is a wide variety of such models, and several alternative formulations exist in the literature. The outline that follows is therefore highly selective.

The Monetary Approach to the Balance of Payments

In general, the theory basically stresses that, under fixed exchange rates, the balance of payments is "essentially a monetary phenomenon." At the simplest analytical level, this follows from the fact that the net balance of international payments is defined in terms of changes in the stock of international reserves that the monetary authorities have at their disposal. First, the approach emphasizes the fact that, irrespective of the composition of the overall balance of payments, its analysis requires that account be taken of money market equilibrium or disequilibrium. A second point of emphasis is that there is a direct link between the balance of payments and the money supply. This is related to the fact, emphasized in Chapter 3, that international reserves constitute one of the more important elements of the money base.

The approach is essentially a theoretical construct or narrow economic model, which is based on a well-defined relationship between the balance of payments, money, and prices, with a definitive role assigned to the demand for and supply of money. In other words, it looks at disturbances in the economy as they affect the balance of payments and prices, and these are in turn interpreted through their effects on the demand for and supply of money. In this context, the approach relies on the general monetarist assumption for a closed economy, that the demand function for money is relatively stable and predictable. In the case of the open economy, the assumption is that, given real incomes, any excess money creation by the banking system will generate changes in international reserves, and therefore a balance-of-payments deficit.

The underlying case for the open economy is that the nominal quantity of money can be changed through balance-of-payments surpluses and deficits, since the latter are considered equivalent to imports and exports of domestic currency. This implies that any internal disparities that arise between the demand for and supply of money are correctible through the balance of payments. In such an environment, the monetary authorities are presumed to have no direct control over the total money supply, but only that portion which is created domestically, especially by the central banking authorities. One implication is that monetary policy should be based on the need to monitor closely the internal money supply and domestic credit expansion.

IMF stabilization programs are in the main influenced by its own version of the monetary approach to the balance of payments, as developed by Polak and other analysts (IMF 1977). The Fund's version is based on a set of more or less simple models the bare bones of which can be outlined as follows. First, heavy reliance is placed on the familiar quantity theory of money identity, in which national income or output equals the money supply multiplied by the velocity of circulation. Second, the money supply is defined as equal to domestic credit plus foreign exchange reserves. Third, the balance of payments is equal to the balance of trade and capital imports, with the behavior of the latter variable independent of the money stock and money incomes. Fourth, the trade balance depends on income, via the propensity to import and not on expenditure. This implies that the money stock is in continuous equilibrium, with income in the current period equal to incomes in previous time periods. Fifth, nominal income is determined by the money stock, with changes in the latter dependent on changes either in domestic credit creation or in foreign exchange reserves. The implication is that, if the money supply is held constant, any growth in domestic credit must be offset by a reduction in foreign exchange reserves, with any such reduction considered tantamount to a balance-of-payments deficit.

Sixth, the transmission process takes place in terms of the influence of the money stock on the level of money income. An increase in domestic credit raises the money stock and therefore money income. First, this leads to a reduction in international reserves and a balance-of-payments deficit. In future rounds, the deficit leads to a decrease in the money stock, and hence money income, until the initial equilibrium is restored. While in some versions of the model exports affect income directly, the main transmission takes place through the flow of international reserves and their respective influence on the money supply and income.

The model's basic conclusion, therefore, is that balance-of-payments deficits occur because domestic credit expansion must be offset by reductions in international reserves. This must follow if money and income are to remain in equilibrium. The policy conclusion, which continues to influence IMF stabilization programs, is that balance-of-payments disequilibria are correctible by limiting the expansion of domestic credit.

The Law of One Price

The monetary approach to the balance of payments is also complemented by aspects of "global monetarism," with certain assumptions common to both approaches. One such assumption is inherent in the "law of one price." This law assumes that there is perfect arbitrage in the international goods market, and that the domestic price level is determined by the international price level or exchange rate. It can be formulated as follows:

$$P_d = EP_f \hspace{4cm} 5.1$$

where P_d is the domestic price level (e.g., Jamaican dollars); E is the exchange rate (e.g., Jamaican dollars per US dollar); and P_f is the foreign price level (US dollars).

The model's theoretical and policy implications for economic stabilization have been well documented. First, in those circumstances where the law of one price can be presumed to hold, the domestic price level is completely determined by the foreign price level. The purest theoretical case explaining this is typified by an economy in which all goods are traded internationally, that is, where nontraded or home goods are nonexistent. In such a case, the internal rate of inflation will be uniquely determined by the external rate of inflation and changes in the exchange rate. The exchange rate therefore becomes a primary stabilization tool, since it bears a direct and unique relationship to the domestic rate of inflation.

However, the influence is considered to be much more indirect when some form of realism is introduced into the model, such as when the presence of nontraded or home goods is taken into account. In the latter case, the effect of exchange rate changes on the price of nontraded goods is assumed to take place through substitution effects, changes in expectations, or both.

Within the more general context of the orthodox demand management approach, the law of one price can be interpreted in terms of imbalances between aggregate demand and supply. As alluded to in Chapter 3, the assumption is that such imbalances are caused by too high a rate of domestic absorption in relation to a country's income, and by the pursuit of macroeconomic policies incompatible with the economy's capacity to produce. In this context, such imbalances are considered a reflection of the fact that domestic prices and costs have moved out of line with international prices. The reasoning, further elaborated in Chapter 6, is that such distortions in relative prices tend to reduce the overall competitiveness of the economy and the efficiency of the resource allocation process. One remedy advocated in this case is the adjustment of the exchange rate or devaluation.

It should be mentioned that the full employment assumption seems to be critical to the monetarist approach, especially in its stricter forms, since it represents one of the mechanisms through which internal and external equilibrium may be attained. In theory, where there is full employment of domestic resources, both the exchange rate and relative prices in the domestic economy will find their appropriate equilibrium levels, and an overall balance-of-payments equilibrium will be assured. In such a situation, the law of one price will hold; domestic currency prices will broadly reflect the ratio of domestic prices to world prices, thereby allowing for the production of traded and nontraded goods in their most profitable proportions.

The Law of One Interest Rate

A second intellectual pillar supporting global monetarism is the "law of one interest rate." It states that the domestic interest rate is equal to the international or foreign interest rate plus a rate of exchange depreciation and another term that captures the effects of disturbances caused by transaction costs, uncertainty, and so on. The law may be stated symbolically, as follows:

$$I_d = I_f + \frac{\Delta E}{E} + a \qquad\qquad 5.2$$

where I_d is the domestic interest rate (e.g., in Jamaica); I_f is the foreign interest rate (e.g., in the United States); $\Delta E/E$ is the rate of exchange depreciation; and a is the disturbance term.

In essence, the law of one interest rate is a theoretical construct that highlights some of the factors that link capital markets at the international level. It also has implications for the types of financial policies that developing countries are supposed to follow. One such implication is that interest rates in developing countries should be at least as high as those obtaining in world capital markets; or, more fundamentally, that interest rates, corrected for foreign exchange expectations, should be higher in developing countries compared to developed ones.

One rationale for this policy prescription is based on perceptions about the differential rates of return on capital in the two types of economies. The reasoning is that the rate of return on capital in developing countries should be higher than that encountered in their more developed counterparts, because of the relative scarcity of capital in the former group of countries compared to the latter. In other cases, high interest rates are justified on the ground that developing countries need to attract foreign capital. These arguments are examined more fully in Chapter 6, which discusses issues related to interest rate reform and financial liberalization.

THE GENERAL SCOURGE OF MONETARISM

The monetarist perspective has come under increasing attack in recent times (see, for example, Kaldor 1982; Blackwell 1978). Besides the more general theoretical and empirical problems posed by the monetarist philosophy, there is a more specific problem about its relevance in a development context. In the latter context, attention is sometimes drawn to what is perceived to be an "anti-development" bias of the monetarist approach.

One problem with monetarism concerns measurement—what constitutes the stock of money. How the money supply is defined has proved problematic for both developed and developing countries. In the former case, money includes a wide spectrum of liquid financial assets which are close substitutes for money defined in a narrower sense. When the money supply is viewed in this broad sense of liquidity, including narrow money and near substitutes for money, it becomes increasingly difficult for the monetary authorities to control it through the use of traditional monetary instruments such as changing the discount rate and the reserve requirements of commercial banks. The same is true for developing countries, but for different reasons. In the latter case, the relatively unsophisticated nature of financial markets means that there are relatively few liquid financial assets that can be readily substituted for money. However, as alluded to in the previous chapter, a possible substitution exists between money, narrowly defined, and the holding of real assets such as property, houses and land, gold and jewelry, stocks of agricultural commodities, consumer durables, and so on.

Second, no a priori judgments can be made about the relationship between changes in the money supply and the behavior of variables in the real sector of the economy. Even if the money supply can be controlled (e.g., if the growth of the money supply is held at a constant level), the behavior of current output, aggregate production, and/or prices might change due to certain independent influences. The latter result is a likely possibility if, for example, there are any significant changes in the propensity to consume, thriftiness, or investment opportunities.

A third problem with monetarism concerns the differential impact of money supply growth in a rapidly growing economy compared to its impact in one operating below its potential capacity. It is evident that for an economy operating at full or nearly full employment levels, with correspondingly high degrees of capacity utilization, any increase in money supply tends to be inflationary. However, where an economy is operating well below capacity, as is especially true for many developing countries, an increase in the money supply can stimulate output growth without unsustainable inflation. Of course, monetarists believe that all forms of inflation are caused by increases in the money supply. However, cost-induced inflation tends to be much more prevalent in a large number of countries. This poses a particularly paradoxical situation for economies operating well below capacity, especially if cost inflation is attacked by orthodox demand management policies that are basically deflationary in nature.

A fourth area of concern relates to the assumptions, explicit or implicit, that are made in some monetarist models about the inflation/unemployment tradeoff. In this context, monetarists generally advocate a slow growth in the money supply, based not only on the possible inflationary consequences of such a policy, but also on the belief that it is impossible to sustain any unemployment level below some "natural rate." Most unemployment is considered to be of a voluntary nature, and the concern with direct employment creation is therefore of secondary importance. This prescription is at odds with the experience of many developing as well as developed countries where there is a prevalence of involuntary, structural, and other forms of unemployment and underemployment. The evidence suggests that these forms of unemployment cannot be solved by orthodox demand management or monetarist policies. It should also be reiterated that the need for raising employment levels is explicitly stated in the IMF's Articles of Agreement. It is also considered a fundamental objective of development from the perspective of this study.

Turning to the specific case of developing countries, a pertinent question concerns the appropriate role of money and traditional monetary instruments as short-term stabilization devices. The conventional instruments include the discount rate, open market operations, and changing the reserve requirements of commercial banks. Even when these instruments are available, monetary authorities in developing countries find it difficult to exercise meaningful control over the money stock because of the well-known structural and institutional rigidities that exist in financial markets.

As indicated in Chapter 4, various forms of dualism and market segmentation still persist in the overall economic structure of many developing countries. In the typical case, the traditional sector is virtually outside the influence of the formal banking sector, and the industrial or modern sector, while susceptible to some degree of influence, remains extremely small. Not only do substantial differences exist between interest rates in organized and unorganized markets, but there is also a general lack of integration between money and capital markets. As emphasized earlier, a large part of the money stock is held in the form of currency or real assets, so that the money supply becomes a largely endogenous variable depending on the public's preference for cash over real assets.

The presence of the above factors leads us to believe that there may be a basic asymmetry governing the implementation of monetary policy in many developing countries. Expansionary monetary policies may be easy to implement, but, but the reverse may prove to be much more difficult. Given the structural and institutional factors mentioned earlier, if a government decides to increase the money supply (e.g., as a means of financing its budget deficit), a substantial part of this expansion is likely to be diverted into the unorganized sector, or otherwise channelled into real asset accumulation, hoarding, and/or speculation. On the contrary, where credit restraints are imposed, the effects are likely to be felt primarily in those sectors using the official or organized money market, with minimal impact on the unorganized sector. The direct impact of restrictive monetary policy is likely to be felt by the relatively small number of growth and development-oriented sectors of the economy.

PART III

THE NEW ORTHODOXY OF TRADE AND FINANCIAL LIBERALIZATION

6

The Liberalization of
Trade and Exchange Regimes

The policy–theoretical framework outlined in Part II represents, in varying degrees, the standard stock-in-trade of analysts who utilize the orthodox demand management approach to economic stabilization. The basic philosophy underlying *stabilization* stems from the general concern for restoring general macroeconomic equilibrium, in the face of disequilibria in the balance of payments, between aggregate demand and supply, savings and investment, government revenue and expenditure, and ultimately, between the demand for and supply of money.

In more recent times, the approach has been complemented by a "new orthodox" policy paradigm predicted on the need for *liberalization* of the trade and exchange regimes of developing countries. In this case, the requisite policy framework is primarily concerned with resource allocation and structural adjustment over the medium- and longer-term horizon. As emphasized in Chapter 2, the need to combine short-term demand management with longer-term policies designed to improve supply capacity reflects a shift in the IMF's policy orientation in the direction of supply management as well as the philosophy underlying the World Bank's structural adjustment lending. The philosophy underlying the new thrust toward liberalization has also received considerable theoretical and empirical support from an impressive and growing number of studies conducted by individual scholars, as well as from research under the auspices of organizations such as the National Bureau of Economic Research, the Organization for Economic Cooperation and Development, the US Agency for International Development, and the World Bank, among others.

The liberalization policy thrust is predicated on the need to remove, on a systematic basis, the multiplicity of distortions and interventions embedded in the economic fabric of developing nations. The study of the related mechanisms through which these distortions operate raises questions not only of an economic nature (i.e., those concerned with allocative efficiency and growth), but also much deeper ones connected with development ideology, the role of markets and government intervention in the development process, how incomes are distributed, and the nature of political institutions.

THEORY AND MEASUREMENT CRITERIA

A foremost question surrounding the liberalization ethic concerns the decision rules that should be used to guide the choice of an optimal mix of trade and exchange policies, and, in particular, the sets of prices and levels of protection that can help to promote feasible national and sectoral goals. The new liberalization orthodoxy views the problem primarily from the standpoint of efficiency and cheapness. In this context, the concepts of "distortion" and "price incentives" are interpreted in terms of those prices that would exist if essentially free domestic markets were to interact with international markets without constraint. These constraints refer to a variety of price and nonprice interventions, including tariffs, quotas, export subsidies, and fixed exchange rates.

The correct policy choice is therefore considered to be one guided by the free market norm, and by a set of "efficiency prices." The latter are considered to be those that adequately reflect the opportunity cost of resources used; or, alternatively, those that result in cost minimization per unit of output, or profit maximization per unit of input use. As mentioned above, such prices are deemed to exist if domestic markets are allowed to interact freely with international markets, without the constraints imposed by various types of private and public interventions in the domestic market. In terms of our previous discussion of global monetarism, the inherent logic is one that supports the ideal "law of one price."

The efficiency norms are firmly grounded in the traditional arguments for the optimalization of free trade. In this context, the conventional wisdom teaches that optimum resource allocation requires equality between the marginal rate of transformation (MRT) of commodities produced domestically and the MRT through trade, as well as equality between these rates of transformation and the corresponding marginal rates of substitution (MRS) in consumption. Further, these rates must be equal to the ratios of prices for the commodities concerned.

These theoretical constructs have come to influence a policy tradition of using world prices as a benchmark for a set of efficiency prices—for measuring the optimum allocation of resources, and the distortions observable in trade and exchange regimes. Such world prices are considered a true gauge of potential earnings from exported output, as well as the potential cost of foreign exchange in the case of imports. World market prices are therefore used to estimate the degree of "distortion" in domestic prices, as well as the comparative cost advantage that a given country might have in international trade.

The underlying reasoning is that the opportunity cost of a resource in any given use is measurable, at the margin, in terms of its actual and potential contribution to a country's foreign trade and balance of payments. The related decision rule is that countries should choose production and investment decisions that will enhance their foreign trade position. Accordingly, the opportunity cost of resource use to a given economy is defined in terms of the alternative possibilities offered for trading with the rest of the world.

Little and Mirlees (1974) justify the use of world prices on the grounds that developing countries are far from optimizing their world trade. The use of world prices in place of domestic market prices is also rationalized on the grounds that, for internationally traded goods (exports and imports), the relevant world prices can be readily identified. This is because they represent prices actually paid in international transactions, that is, payments for imports and receipts for exports. In addition, it is relatively easier to find the world price for a commodity, compared to its domestic price, since the former price can easily be found in published sources.

Many of the empirical studies that attempt to measure the effects of price distortions and the system of agricultural and industrial incentives prevailing in developing countries make explicit or implicit use of some notion of world prices as a proxy for the system of efficiency prices. From an analytic perspective, most of these studies measure the effects of trade intervention and agricultural and industrial incentives by utilizing concepts such as effective and nominal rates of protection and domestic resource costs. Some of these measures are briefly defined below, and implications for the liberalization argument highlighted.

Nominal and Effective Protection

First, there is the nominal rate of protection, which connotes the extent to which the ex-factory or ex-farmgate price of a domestically produced commodity diverges from the international price of the same or equivalent product, because of the duties and taxes affecting imports and exports. The relevant measure, in this case, is the nominal protection coefficient (NPC) which is a ratio measure of the disparity between domestic prices and international prices, with the latter expressed in terms of "border prices" (international prices converted into their domestic currency equivalent).

The NPC therefore measures the extent to which export commodities are taxed or, alternatively, the extent to which domestic producers are offered protection from world markets (subsidized). It is a static measure, and only captures the divergence between domestic and international prices at a given point in time. In symbolic terms, the NPC can be defined as follows:

$$NPC_i = P_i^d / P_i^b \qquad\qquad 6.1$$

where NPC_i is the nominal protection coefficient for the ith commodity; P_i^d is the domestic price of the ith commodity; and P_i^b is the border price of the ith commodity.

To elaborate, if a domestic industry is protected by, say, a 50 percent duty on competing imports, nominal protection to its domestic sales would approximate 50 percent. In the case of an export industry subject to a 50 percent export tax on the f.o.b. price, nominal protection would be minus 50 percent. In situations where exports are not subject to any export taxation, nominal protection would be zero.

In most countries, discrepancies usually arise between international and domestic prices for final goods as well as for inputs used in the production process. In such cases, the emphasis is on measuring value added per unit of output, which refers to the value that is added through the production process, over and above the value of traded inputs. This follows in the tradition of the theory of effective protection, which postulates that the quantity of a commodity that a given producer decides to produce depends on the net margins he or she expects to receive (Balassa et al. 1971; Corden 1971).

In this context, the relevant measure is the effective protection rate (EPR), which specifically takes into account the nominal protection affecting both inputs and outputs. The effective rate of protection can be measured directly, or by using the effective protection coefficient (EPC), which is defined as the ratio of value added in production measured in domestic prices to value added measured in international prices.

The effective protection coefficient can be defined in the following manner:

$$\text{EPC}_i = \frac{P_i^d - \sum_{j=1}^{k} (a_{ij} \cdot P_j^d)}{P_i^b - \sum_{j=1}^{k} (a_{ij} \cdot P_j^b)} \qquad 6.2$$

where P_i^d is the domestic price of the ith output; a_{ij} is the quantity of the jth input used to produce one unit of the ith output; P_j^d is the domestic price of the jth input; P_i^b is the border price of the ith output; P_j^b is the border price of the jth input; and $j = 1 \ldots k$ (i.e., all traded inputs).

In simpler terms,

$$\text{EPC} = \frac{(\text{Domestic value of output}) - (\text{Cost of inputs at domestic prices})}{(\text{World value of output}) - (\text{Cost of the same inputs at international prices})}$$

or

$$EPC = \frac{\text{Domestic value added}}{\text{World value added}}$$

The EPC can also be expressed in terms of the EPR, as follows:

$$EPR = \frac{(\text{Domestic value added}) - (\text{World value added})}{\text{World value added}} \times 100$$

$$= (EPC - 1) \times 100$$

Assuming that border prices reflect a country's trading opportunities, other things being equal, the effective protection given a particular economic activity provides an indication of the economic efficiency of that activity. For example, the economic efficiency of a firm requiring, say, 100 percent effective protection is, prima facie, less than the efficiency of a firm requiring, say, 10 percent effective protection, or one with negative effective protection. Negative effective protection indicates the extent to which the domestic cost of processing a given commodity is less than the cost of the same processes when incorporated in an imported good. By contrast, positive effective protection indicates the extent to which the domestic cost of processing the commodity exceeds the price of buying the same processes when they are used in the production of an imported good.

In terms of empirical interpretation, an NPC value of greater than one of a given commodity indicates that it is being subsidized, and the greater the value, the higher the subsidy. By contrast, an NPC of less than one indicates that the commodity in question is being taxed, and the lower it is, the heavier is the taxation. Like the NPC, the EPC can assume a range of values. An EPC greater than one implies that the producers are enjoying positive protection, that the intervention mechanism is enabling them to receive a return on their resources greater than they would get without such intervention. By contrast, if the EPC is less than one, the producers are receiving negative protection, that is, they are being taxed. In other words, the presumption is that they could have received a high return if they were to face international prices instead of domestic prices for both inputs and outputs.

The available empirical evidence suggests that, in general, the industrial sector in most developing countries receives relatively high nominal and effective rates of protection. Studies by the World Bank and other agencies show that the prices of industrial products in many of these countries range between 30 and 200 percent above world prices, indicating substantially high rates of protection. This is explained, in part, by the strategies of import substitution industrialization that these countries have followed. This aspect is taken up later in this chapter.

By contrast, farmers in several countries tend to receive only 50–80 percent or less of the farmgate equivalent of export prices for their major crops, indicating relatively heavy rates of taxation. The heavy taxation of major export crops is particularly evident in sub-Saharan African countries where export crops have been traditionally marketed by parastatal agencies that do not operate under competitive conditions, and where export receipts in terms of domestic currency tend to be reduced, on account of the influence of overvalued exchange rates (World Bank 1981).

From Protection to Comparative Advantage

While measures of nominal and effective protection do provide some indication of the extent of market intervention, or the potential for exports, they do not indicate whether a country use its resources to produce goods primarily for the home market or for international trade. This depends on the nature of a country's comparative advantage. A country is said to have a comparative advantage in a given commodity when it can produce that commodity relatively efficiently in comparison to other commodities and/or countries (whether the same land, labor, or capital might produce more value added if they were used to produce something else), and whether it might be profitable to expand the production of the commodity, and to what extent.

The relevant empirical measure in this case is the domestic resource cost coefficient (DRC) which compares the relative costs of import-competing goods to the foreign exchange earned on exports. In other words, the DRC coefficient measures the cost of domestic resources (land, labor, materials, etc.) that are used to earn or save a net unit of foreign exchange. In analytical terms, it is the ratio of primary factors of production, valued at efficiency or border prices, to value added in border prices.

$$\text{DRC} = \frac{\sum_{j=k+1}^{n} a_j V_j}{P^b - \sum_{j=1}^{k} a_j P_j^b} \qquad\qquad 6.3$$

where a_j is the amount of nontraded input j per unit of output; V_j is the domestic opportunity cost of nontraded input j, converted into its border price equivalent; P^b is the border price of output; P_j^b is the border price of input j; $j = 1 \ldots k$, representing traded inputs; and $k + 1 \ldots n =$ nontraded inputs.

The DRC can assume a range of numerical values, and a ranking of these values is indicative of different levels of efficiency, or of the international competitiveness of domestic production. A DRC value of less than one indicates efficiency and international competitiveness. The implication is that the economy saves foreign exchange from local production, since the opportunity cost of its domestic resources is less than the net foreign exchange it gains from exports, or saves from import substituting activities. In the reverse case, where the DRC is greater than one, the economy is incurring costs in terms of net foreign exchange, in excess of what it gains or saves from domestic production.

At this stage, at least three general comments can be made about the use of DRCs and related measures as guides to the design of optimal production and trade strategies. First, the evidence shows that many developing countries still maintain a strong comparative advantage for a wide range of food and export crops. The same is true for certain industrial products. However, especially in the case of agriculture, a combination of factors tends to militate against their maintaining this relatively favorable position. As discussed in more detail in the next section of the chapter, these include the general neglect of the agricultural sector, the lack of adequate incentives, and poor planning.

Second, even where strong comparative advantage is indicated, many developing countries face trade barriers and international trading arrangements that increase the difficulties of expanding certain traditional exports and diversifying into new areas that offer better prospects. These include the escalation of tariffs on semiprocessed products and nontariff barriers on certain livestock and agricultural commodities. However, this does not obviate the need for these countries to introduce more efficiency into their production process.

The third area of comment is methodological in nature, and concerns the fact that the DRC and related measures are static efficiency ones that show comparative advantage at a particular point in time. They fail to capture the dynamic possibilities that might arise through changes in price relationships, input costs, and technologies. Further, they do not sufficiently take into account certain external benefits that may be associated with the production process, such as those related to demand and production linkages, and employment creation.

SOME SYSTEMATIC EFFECTS OF DISTORTIONS

Developing countries tend to utilize several types of interventionist policy measures as a means of ostensibly satisfying national and sectoral development objectives. An illustrative list is provided in Table 6.1. These include (1) those designed to control trade and exchange, for example, tariffs, restrictions or prohibitions on imports accompanied by comprehensive import licensing systems, and various taxes; (2) fixed producer and consumer prices; and (3) various forms of intervention into input pricing, such as price subsidies (incentive pricing), and taxes (disincentive pricing).

The general consensus is that the various interventionist policy measures have emerged out of a situation in which policymakers in the

Table 6.1 *Price intervention typologies schematized*

Intervention typology	Characteristic features
Trade and exchange controls	Means of controlling domestic prices and/or generating government revenue. Export taxes, import restrictions, subsidies, export and import controls cause domestic prices to diverge from world prices.
Exchange rate overvaluation	Changes in relative prices; exports taxed and consumption of imported goods subsidized.
Export/import quotas and tariffs	Used to discourage imports, capture surplus from exports, generate government revenue, and protect domestic industry.
Taxes	Mechanisms to generate government revenue, improve income distribution profile, and change pattern of resource allocation.
Fixed prices	Various types: maximum producer prices, ceilings on consumer prices, freezing of wholesale and retail price margins, and commodity price supports.
Producer prices	Maximum prices for export crops set by monopolistic parastatal agencies. Indirect tax on producers because purchased commodities usually sold above fixed maximum price paid producers. Used to provide stabilization in markets experiencing fluctuations, and generate government revenue.
Consumer prices	Retail prices controlled by law, through use of ceiling or fixed prices. Sometimes combined with import duties to discourage consumption of controlled items.
Price margins	Wholesale/retail margins fixed by law. Divergence usually noticed between final consumer prices and cost due to transportation, seasonal variations, and quality differentials.
Commodity prices	Selected commodities purchased at guaranteed minimum price. Objectives to encourage domestic production, maintain farmers' income, and price stabilization by keeping prices above some minimum threshold level.
Input pricing	Various types: free market pricing, price subsidies (incentive pricing), or taxes (disincentive pricing).
Price subsidies	Input subsidies may be used to encourage domestic production of specific commodities (product specific subsidies), or to encourage the use of specific inputs (adoption pricing), or alternatively, to guarantee the continued use of modern inputs, especially when world market prices are fluctuating. Subsidies also provided to maintain a fixed ratio between input and output prices, and/or fixed terms of trade between agriculture and supply industries (fixed ratio pricing).
Taxes or disincentive pricing	Prices of inputs set above those obtaining in open markets. Objectives to discourage the use of certain inputs (e.g., highly capital-intensive ones), protect certain domestic industries, or generate tax revenues.

Source: Compiled by author.

70

developing countries perceived the choices available to them primarily in terms of a dichotomy between export promotion (EP) and import substitution (IS). As a result, the general pattern of development from the 1950s through the 1970s was typified by heavy protection, mainly of IS industries, and a concomitant bias against agriculture, and/or old or new export industries.

The systematic effects of the related trade and exchange restrictions are now well documented (Bhagwati 1978; Krueger 1978; World Bank 1981). It is generally agreed that as countries moved from strategies based on heavy import restrictions and overvalued exchange rates to more open economies and exchange rates closer to equilibrium levels, they found it easier to step up the pace of export, and therefore GNP growth. The relevant evidence suggests that countries that have pursued export-oriented growth strategies have, in general, experienced higher rates of economic growth than others that have relied on more inward-looking types of import substitution industrialization.

The most commonly cited examples are the "success story" trade development countries of Southeast Asia, South Korea, Taiwan, and Hong Kong, and what are perceived to be "newly industrializing countries," such as Brazil and the Ivory Coast. These countries are now being widely cited as models of development. This has also resulted in an increasing demand by some member countries of the IMF and World Bank for information and advice that would help to pave the way for introduction of reforms into their system of agricultural and industrial incentives.

To continue the story, the evidence also suggests that the countries that relied on inward-looking strategies generally failed to liberalize their trade and exchange regimes. As a result, their economic performance was poor, and they found it difficult in adjusting their balance of payments in the face of external shocks. These difficulties, in turn, forced them to borrow excessively in world capital markets.

The relatively poor economic performance associated with IS compared to EP strategies has, in general, been attributed to the effects of various price and cost distortions that have accompanied trade and exchange regimes. In this context, most studies emphasize the negative consequences of overvalued exchanged rates and import restrictions. First, an overvalued exchange rate means that the foreign currency obtained for exports can be converted into a relatively small amount of domestic currency. Overvaluation basically implies that the exchange rate is above some "equilibrium" level which balances the demand and supply for foreign exchange. When this occurs, exports are taxed and imports are subsidized. Lowering the exchange rate, for example, by devaluing the domestic currency, raises the domestic price of traded goods. This gives a premium to exports and taxes the consumption of imported goods. We return to this subject in the next chapter.

Second, and in the case of import restrictions, the relevant effects can be illustrated in terms of the mechanisms by which import licenses are allocated to potential recipients, and the differential effects on resource allocation that result from this practice. As Krueger (1974) indicates, such practices generally lead to various forms of "rent seeking" behavior. Such rent seeking arises because the receipt of the import license constitutes an extremely valuable property right, and potential claimants are therefore willing to devote resources—at times considerable—in the attempt to capture this valuable property right.

Krueger and others have identified several types of rent-seeking behavior. One type is associatcd with the system used for licensing imports of consumer goods in some developing countries. In this case, competition for rents normally occurs through entry into the wholesaler-imported business by smaller-than-average retail establishments, which are able to maintain operations at economically low and inefficient levels. This is because of the relatively high markups on the individual items they sell. The high profit earned on individual items is usually sufficient to keep the business afloat. The point is that the resources used on sales on imported and other commodities are considerably higher than they would be if the establishments were of a more optimal size.

A second example of rent-seeking behavior can be found where import licenses for raw materials and intermediate goods are allocated in proportion to firms' capacities in relation to total industrial capacity. When this happens, firms are tempted to add to their capacity, even though idle capacity may exist. This is because the additional benefits that are derivable from import licenses may exceed by far the rate of return on alternative investments. This type of rent seeking helps to explain the high levels of idle capacity that can be observed in several developing countries.

Another form of rent-seeking behavior occurs because government officials are usually the ones who make decisions about respective allocations. In this case, substantial resources may be expended by potential recipients in the attempt to influence the allocative process in their favor, through bribery, hiring relatives of officials, and so on.

While rent seeking constitutes both legal and illegal activities, it is usually analyzed in terms of legality. However, it is now recognized that the relatively high levels of protection afforded some types of economic activity in developing countries tend to provide sizable gains to those who can circumvent regulations. As a result, there has developed a considerable number of illegal transactions in goods and currency, marked by practices such as the under- and over-invoicing of exports and imports, smuggling, and black markets in goods and foreign exchange.

In the typical case, the foreign exchange market reveals a dual structure which is dichotomized into a legal or official market on the one hand, and a "black" or "parallel" market on the other, with each submarket having its own foreign exchange rate. The parallel market is usually associated with various forms of illegal activities, which are the result of legal restrictions put on the exchange of money.

There are various sources of demand for black market foreign exchange. One type stems from the existence of low or negative real interest rates. In this case, the black market foreign exchange is used as a store of value abroad, and is therefore sought as a means of purchasing assets denominated in foreign currencies. Second, the black market foreign exchange may be used to purchase foreign goods for smuggling into a country. As a result, the user of such foreign exchange is able to avoid the cost of tariffs and, given the transaction and other costs associated with smuggling, capture the tariff and/or tarriff equivalent of quotas. In other cases, the black market foreign exchange may be used to finance additional purchases of legally importable goods. Both types of transactions can lead to a misallocation of resources, in the sense that the purchaser of foreign exchange in each case is able to earn higher-than-normal profits by selling these goods at a higher price domestically.

However, the activities mentioned above transcend the foreign exchange market. In many countries, they have now become an integral part of a vibrant, and much more pervasive, parallel economy. National accounts statistics do not usually include these types of activities. The parallel economy has expanded to such an extent in some countries that official figures bear little relation to what is actually taking place in the economy.

The author's random observance of the parallel economy in a few African and Caribbean countries reveals that the related transactions have both productive and distributive functions. Examples of production activities include the growing of coffee, cocoa, and other crops for illegal exportation, or otherwise for smuggling across national frontiers . This practice is common in most West African countries where parastatal agencies are the sole buying agencies of major export crops, and where low producer prices and overvalued exchange rate tend to depress farmers' potential receipts in terms of domestic currency. Another example is the growing of banned crops such as marijuana (ganja) in Jamaica, due to the relatively high profitability attached to this activity.

The distributive activities of the parallel economy include various forms of corruption, theft, smuggling, and middlemen activities for acquiring scarce commodities. All segments of the population participate, more or less, in these activities. The activities of the parallel economy not only provide additional sources of income and employment, but, in many cases, they are the only means of subsistence. In other cases, they represent an avenue of upward mobility for those who can successfully exploit the opportunities offered.

The evidence, though tentative, also suggests that activities in the parallel economy represent evasion of control by the state, and political control by the bureaucratic class. A common belief in some countries is that select members of this group attempt to monopolize the parallel market for themselves, by means of personal connections or otherwise by restricting access to scarce resources. However, it is also likely that such groups have found it impossible to extend their control sufficiently, and therefore cannot monopolize the parallel economy, as they have the official economy. In the latter case, one mechanism of control that is often used is through the process of parastatal intervention. This aspect is taken up below.

We now turn to a consideration of interventions that take place through the practice of fixing (maximum and minimum) producer prices. These types of interventions are especially relevant to the viability of the agricultural sector. In a large number of cases, prices are either set by law, or by official purchasing agencies (parastatals or marketing boards), which control all or a significant share of the market in order to set such prices. In the majority of cases, such institutions are the sole buying agencies for many export crops, and usually have complete control over exports and imports.

The practice of fixing producer prices at relatively low levels (in relation to world prices) explains, in part, the relatively high levels of taxation of export crops alluded to earlier. However, mention should be made of some of the historical circumstances governing the evolution of such policies. First, the monocultural production structure that most developing countries inherited from their colonial past meant that the taxation of export crops provided the easiest and most obvious source of government revenue. Second, since the world market demand for most of these crops tends to be inelastic, it was a reasonable judgment that such policies would help to improve the countries' terms of trade on world markets.

As indicated earlier, while most developing countries would seem to have a short-run comparative advantage in terms of agricultural exports, they might have been forced to give special attention to industry on account of the secular fluctuations in the world prices of primary commodities that they export, as well as the apparent downward trend of primary products compared to industrial products. Many countries might have used fixed producer prices as a means of stabilizing prices and incomes in markets that experience wide fluctuations.

However, the more recent experience, especially in African countries, suggests that there have been efforts to reduce the traditionally high levels of taxation on export crops. Producer prices have been raised in a number of countries, thereby significantly altering the historical relationship between relatively low official producer prices and higher world prices. In some cases, these producer prices have reached levels significantly above the corresponding world prices. In other cases, however, such increases were not large enough when compared to the corresponding import prices (Christensen and Witucki 1982; World Bank 1984a).

While many countries have been taking steps aimed at liberalizing their trade and exchange regimes, the low producer prices still form part of a wide range of "administered prices," including interest rates and critical consumer and factor prices, which continue to be maintained below their true economic levels. While such pricing policies might have helped to contain the rise in domestic prices in the short run, the general result has been damage to the investment and production potential of the economy.

The most damaging effects of such policies, especially in sub-Saharan Africa, are traceable to the stagnation and decline in agricultural production. For both food and export commodities, the combined effects of overvalued exchange rates and low producer prices have produced a systematic bias against their production. As indicated in the previous section of the chapter, many producers of food items as well as traditional export crops find that they are not paid enough to cover production costs, even for those crops for which they have a strong comparative advantage.

Inflexible exchange rates, low producer prices, and relatively low duties on food imports have also encouraged the dependence on such imports at the expense of domestic production of local grains and root crops. A typical case is Nigeria, where imports of wheat and rice accounted for over 80 percent of net commercial imports during the 1970s. Nigeria is also a classic example of the "Dutch disease," the adverse effects on agriculture of booming oil and mineral sectors. The net result of this process is that resources are drawn away from food production and agriculture generally, and toward the nontradeable goods sector. A further result is the development of high per capita income zones, leading to a higher propensity to import "preferred" or "convenience" foods such as wheat and rice.

Policies to control the price of basic foodstuffs have also proved self-defeating. They have succeeded, by and large, in securing only a limited supply of low-priced, and often low-quality, foodstuffs for a relatively small group of urban consumers, and often at the expense of the urban and rural poor. Further, such policies have tended to increase farmers' and traders' risks in producing and marketing surpluses. In addition, they have failed to stabilize, and in many cases, may have actually destabilized supplies over the course of the production cycle.

As emphasized earlier in the chapter, the system of protection might have been responsible for a distorted pattern of industrial development, by encouraging the development of a high-cost, import-intensive, and relatively capital-intensive industrial structure. The industries that have been encouraged (mainly of the packaging and assembly-type variety) have produced very few benefits for the economy in the form of foreign exchange, employment, or skill development, and might have discouraged the development of local industries that rely on local raw material and labor.

In many cases, the highly protective tariff structure has led to a distorted form of urban development, and to the neglect of the rural sector.

The adoption of highly capital-intensive techniques have been accompanied, in many instances, by high wages paid to well-organized urban elites. In general, these effects have been reinforced by government policies that deliberately kept the price for food, energy, and other supplies to urban groups at low levels.

The overall effect has been the subsidization of modern elites at the expense of the poor. The general conclusion is that the rural and agricultural sectors have been taxed in favor of a relatively high-cost, high-wage, and high-profit, import-substituting, and domestically oriented manufacturing sector. The overall result has been a squeezing of the poor and powerless, and a general nurturing of a domestic industrial and bureaucratic class earning excessive monopoly rents.

Related to this is the fact that the systems of bureaucratic restrictions and interventions have been closely tied to the monopoly power held by state marketing agencies, parastatal organizations, and, in some cases, large national and international firms in the private sector. In a number of countries, these organizations have become the mechanisms through which governments intervene not only in export and import marketing, but also in other important areas of economic life. Many of these organizations originated during the colonial era, and at a time when colonial governments wanted to maintain control over major export commodities and certain strategic internal marketing activities. Some of these institutions were dismantled after independence, but their numbers have increased, and their basic functions were retained, and/or strengthened, in some postcolonial societies.

This practice is usually rationalized on economic grounds, in terms of their potential contribution to government revenue, as well as maintenance of price stability in the face of fluctuations in the prices of major commodity exports. However, the evidence suggests that many parastatals do not operate on a financially sustainable basis, and engage in practices that tend to militate against their commercial viability. This stems, in part, from the nature of the policy directives that they are given, and the fact that they have become subject to the political process, and to the patronage of those with political, social, and administrative power.

A useful example is provided by those organizations that are responsible for marketing agricultural commodities. Some of the factors militating against their economic and financial viability have been well documented. According to the World Bank's study of sub-Saharan Africa (1981), many of the prices that parastatals pay farmers do not reflect transport costs between locations or storage costs between time periods. Uniform "panterritorial" and "pantemporal" prices are often regarded as a political requirement when an official agency is involved. Such prices tend to subsidize distant producers at the expense of those who are nearby, and they conceal transport or storage costs behind relatively high marketing margins or financial losses. In the typical case, such transfers imply that parastatals are burdened with the heavy financial costs associated with long-distance trade and storage, with the more profitable trade cornered by operators in the parallel market.

Second, and as indicated earlier, a large number of the problems relating to parastatals, as well as the general character of government interventions, are of a political nature. In the majority of developing countries, low-income farmers are among some of the least organized and least powerful groups in society. Where particular export commodities are produced to an important degree by groups with more political power, the interests of these producers have often been served by government boards and parastatals.

The general conclusion is that the monopolistic operations of parastatals entail large allocative and social costs, and a highly inequitable transfer of income from the large majority of low-income farmers to government bureaucrats and private capitalists. In addition, the evidence suggests that parastatals, especially in Africa, have been relatively inefficient due to poor management, high domestic transportation costs, and the pressure on marketing margins. As a result, they have required heavy subsidies from the public treasury. The large and unfavorable allocative and distributive effects of these monopolistic agencies have led to an increasing call for substantial reforms and/or their dismantlement, with more of their functions taken over by the private sector.

LIBERALIZATION OF CREDIT MARKETS AND INTEREST RATES

The new orthodoxy of financial liberalization posits the need to introduce financial reforms as a means of improving the environment in which monetary policy takes place, as well as in the overall efficiency and effectiveness of such policy. In particular, it is predicated on the need to reduce, and eventually eliminate, various forms of government intervention in financial markets. This section of the chapter focuses on credit market imperfections and issues relating to interest rate policy.

As indicated in Chapter 4, low and negative real interest rates have become a pervasive feature of underdeveloped financial systems. Advocates of interest rate liberalization or reform point to the various economic costs that are associated with low interest rate policies. Accordingly, a number of theoretical and practical policy criteria have been advanced for reducing these costs, and for improving the efficiency of the system.

Policy makers in developing countries usually defend low interest rate policies on at least three grounds. First, low interest rates are justified in terms of their potential for increasing the low investment, income, and growth levels that typically characterize the economies of developing countries. A second rationale is based on the need to improve the intersectoral allocation of credit and investment, as a means of promoting a more balanced economic structure and growth process. A third rationale is linked to the desire to hold financial costs down. One variation on this theme points to the possible inflationary effects of raising interest rates.

Several theoretical and practical policy arguments have been advanced against a low interest rate policy. As mentioned above, one justification for low interest rates tends to stress their potentially stimulatory effects on investment, income, and growth. First, it can be shown theoretically that a policy of low interest rates may not only inhibit investment, but also reduce the average rate of investment below the maximum attainable rate.

The basis of this argument is the disequilibrium that presumably results between investment demand and its availability on account of low interest rates. As McKinnon (1973) argues, if real interest rates are reduced below market equilibrium levels, the demand for investment is likely to increase, but this may be accompanied by a fall in the actual level of investment. The latter result is likely to occur because, when interest rates are at a relatively low level, an adequate amount of savings will not be forthcoming to finance the induced investment demand.

Accordingly, low interest rates will tend to result in an excess demand for investment. When this occurs, the available investment funds will have to be rationed among all competing investors who are willing to borrow at the depressed rate. Under competitive conditions, the supply of funds by financial intermediaries is usually based on the ranking of rates of return on alternative investments. Such a decision rule cannot be adhered to when there is rationing, and lending rates are controlled. Under such circumstances, the financial decision-making process is not influenced by rational economic criteria, but more by other factors such as political influence and the capacity of potential borrowers to provide collateral.

The second justification for low interest rates concerns the need for reallocating investment resources among various sectors of the economy, as a means of promoting balanced economic growth and improving the social profitability of investment. In this context, policy makers in developing countries point to the emergence of a wide and increasing divergence between the private and social profitability of investment, on account of the past and present practices of financial institutions.

This divergence between private and social profitability of investment can be explained by the following factors: (1) financial institutions either underestimate the credit-worthiness of certain potential investors, or have private costs of assessing credit-worthiness and of administering loans that are higher than their true social costs. In other words, they may tend to overestimate the risk as well as administrative costs of extending loans to certain sectors, such as subsistence agriculture; (2) since the primary concern of private financial institutions is with maximizing private profitability, they do not necessarily take into consideration the external and other benefits that may be associated with the development of certain sectors considered to be "high priority" ones by the national authorities (Johnson 1974).

Selective credit controls are usually the primary weapons used to reallocate credit among sectors, and to encourage or discourage certain types of economic activity as a means of bringing the requirements of private and social profitability closer together. On an overall basis, this selectivity of credit policy is predicated on the assumption that it is possible to influence the pattern of investment and production by differentiating between the cost and availability of investment to different sectors of the economy. A further assumption is that such differentiation can be achieved either by directly controlling the activities of financial institutions, or by providing them with indirect inducements.

In the above context, the allocation of credit can be influenced directly by stipulating the types of loans that financial institutions can make, as well as loan ceilings, interest rate levels, collateral required, and so on. Alternatively, where the central bank exercises some degree of control over the banking system, it may, as a matter of policy, decide to use its control on a selective basis as a means of injecting some differentiation into credit policy. Examples are cases where selective exceptions are made on various reserve requirements, or where different rediscount rates are used for different types of loans.

In general, interest rate liberalization is predicated on the need to reduce the various redistributive, welfare, and other costs that are associated with the use of credit controls to allocate credit for alternative investment purposes. These costs are deemed to occur because credit controls tend to distort the manner in which market forces determine the allocation of real resources. The divergence from market equilibrium occurs because credit controls have effects that are similar to those of implicit tax-cum-subsidy intervention mechanisma.

As Johnson (1974) argues, credit controls represent a mechanism through which sectors considered to be "low priority" are taxed in order to subsidize "high priority" or preferred sectors. The tax subsidy effects usually take place through differential discount rate policies. In addition, such policies tend to have inflationary effects that are themselves important mechanisms for taxing certain sectors and subsidizing others. Further, such policies normally lead to an expansion in the money supply, with restrictions sometimes placed on the ability of the monetary authorities to control it.

The tax-cum-subsidy elements are also reflected by the fact that implicit taxes are imposed on financial institutions and their traditional clients in order to subsidize preferred sectors. Where banks and other financial institutions are forced to lend to preferred sectors, wealth tends to be redistributed toward borrowers in these high-priority sectors. While this may lead to an overall improvement in economic welfare, and especially that of groups who could not participate in the credit market, it may not represent the most rational allocation of resources on efficiency grounds.

Given the disadvantages of low interest rate and related policies, the next question concerns the criteria that should be used in determining appropriate interest rate levels. The liberalization ethic relies, explicitly or implicitly, on theoretical criteria similar to those underlying the "law of one interest rate." However, answers to the problems posed by appropriateness must ultimately depend on how one views interest rates and interest rate policy.

In theory, an interest rate can be viewed as a social rate of discount that determines the optimal allocation of resources between savings and consumption, as well as a rationing device for efficient allocation among alternative forms of investment. Accordingly, the real interest rate is considered a reward for the sacrifice of holding rather than consuming wealth. Based on the assumption that individuals tend to optimize some stream of real consumption/savings over time, the real interest rate can be conceptualized as the relative price between present and future consumption/saving. Under competitive conditions, this relative price will be determined in financial markets by consumers' and savers' time preferences, the level of real income, and the real rate of return over costs.

Defined in this way, the real interest rate becomes an "equilibrium" rate, which is based on the assumption that a perfectly competitive market will ensure an optimal rate of savings and an efficient pattern of investment. Under such circumstances, the structure and level of interest rates would be determined by the free interaction of demand and supply, and would therefore reflect the true economic or opportunity cost of capital.

While the "equilibrium" interest rate is a useful heuristic device, it lacks practical significance. Second, prevailing interest rates in most developing countries tend to diverge from this notional equilibrium rate, due to the large number of market imperfections, externalities, and government interventions found in financial markets. As is well known, capital and output markets in developing countries are highly segmented, and this is reflected in a multiplicity of borrowing and lending rates. This raises the question of whether a uniform equilibrium rate for the entire economy can be used as an approximate index for the availability of funds.

A similar criticism applies to the concept of a "shadow" or "accounting" interest rate, which features highly in the analytical black box of both the World Bank and the IMF. The "shadow" interest rate can be considered a theoretical norm for measuring the degree to which actual interest rates diverge from some optimum level. It provides a broad quideline for measuring the efficiency of resource allocation. As in the case of outputs, "accounting" or "efficiency" prices are used to value major scarce inputs such as foreign exchange and skilled labor.

The practical significance of shadow interest rates has also been questioned on the grounds that it is impossible to identify an optimal rate of interest that can serve as an objective yardstick for determining optimal savings and investment. According to Sen (1961), the choice of an optimal savings rate involves temporal value judgments, since it raises questions about equity between present and future. The same logic seems to apply to the optimum rate of interest. In other words, such a rate cannot be determined on an objective basis, and without recourse to value judgments.

The above difficulties notwithstanding, developing countries still have to make practical policy choices concerning the appropriateness of prevailing interest rates and interest rate policy. In this context, a widely used benchmark in schemes for financial liberalization is that money rates of interest should remain positive in real terms, that is, after deflating their nominal levels by changes in inflation rates. This is required for both lending and deposit rates. The former are viewed as a means of regulating the cost and availability of credit, while deposit rates are considered instruments for mobilizing savings in a monetary form. This objective would be achieved if the interest rates offered on time and savings deposits, claims on financial institutions, and government securities were to be set at sufficiently high levels.

One basic idea underlying the liberalization philosophy is that there should be a relatively low spread between borrowing and lending rates. This spread is usually large in developing countries, reflecting the poorly developed state of the banking system, and government intervention in the financial system. The argument is that, while some of these regulations help to prevent failures of financial intermediaries, they nevertheless prove costly to the financial system. This is because they result in divergences between borrowing and lending rates that are far in excess of what would prevail in a more competitive environment. The idea of reducing the spread between borrowing and lending rates follows, therefore, from the orthodox assumption of equilibrium in competitive markets. Under competitive conditions, the spread between lending rates and the average cost of loanable funds is considered to be just high enough to cover costs, risks, and normal profits. In such a situation, borrowing and lending rates will converge toward some market equilibrium rate.

As mentioned in Chapter 5, one policy implication of the "law of one interest rate" is that interest rates in developing countries should be at least as high, and preferably higher than, those in developed countries. The underlying assumption is that, given the relative scarcity of capital in the former countries, the marginal efficiency and corresponding rate of return on capital should be higher there. The need to attract foreign capital is also used as a justification for such a policy. In the case of the argument based on differential rates of return, there is no conclusive empirical evidence that the marginal efficiency of capital is higher in developing countries. Second, while it may be true that the foreign investment elasticity is somewhat sensitive to interest rate levels in developing countries, it is known that other factors shaping the overall investment climate (e.g., political stability) may play a more instrumental role.

The conclusion that emerges is that no a priori judgments can be made about the criteria that should be used for determining the appropriate level and structure of interest rates in developing countries. While considerations of efficiency are important, the acid test lies in the extent to which the given level and structure of interest rates are synergistic with a country's overall development goals, its investment strategies, and its potential for mobilizing savings. These and other issues pertaining to interest rate policy are extensively discussed in Coats and Khatkhate (1980), pp. 449–629.

7

Exchange Rate Adjustment

One of the most controversial, and indeed complex, aspects of IMF policy packages concerns the inordinate degree of emphasis placed on exchange rate depreciation, or devaluation, especially in those developing countries whose exchange rates are tied to major currencies. In this chapter, an attempt is made to throw some light on the devaluation issue, by considering some of the theoretical and practical policy problems involved with this policy measure.

As indicated in the previous chapter, there has emerged a substantial body of evidence suggesting that exchange rates tend to be overvalued in a large majority of developing countries. In theory, this implies that there is some distortion in the price of foreign exchange, and this is usually measured in terms of some deviation of the prevailing exchange rate from a notional equilibrium value. To reiterate, when the official exchange rate overvalues the domestic currency, exporters receive much less in terms of domestic currency for every unit of foreign exchange earned than they would have if the exchange rate were in equilibrium, that is, if there were a balance in the demand for and supply of foreign exchange. On the other hand, importers tend to pay less for imports in terms of domestic currency than they would have with an equilibrium rate.

In other words, an overvalued currency represents an implicit tax on exports and an implicit subsidy on imports. It tends to reduce export competitiveness, encourages import dependence, and is typically accompanied by a legion of distortions in the domestic production structure. Accordingly, the need for exchange rate adjustment is usually advocated in terms of using an exchange rate that gives a more realistic valuation of domestic currency in terms of foreign currency—one that removes the implicit tax, subsidy, and related distortionary effects.

DETERMINING THE APPROPRIATE EXCHANGE RATE

Since recommendations for devaluation are usually based on some belief or conviction that the prevailing exchange rate is inappropriate, we begin by considering some alternative views on the question of appropriateness. In ideal terms, appropriateness is usually conceptualized in terms of the notion of an equilibrium exchange rate. This equilibrium rate is considered to be one that, under full employment conditions, and with all price distortions removed, would result in overall balance-of-payments equilibrium. Implicit in the attainment of this equilibrium is a time dimension, which is assumed to be that period of time necessary for various price and output adjustments to be fully realized.

One assumption underlying this theory is that the divergence between prevailing exchange rates and the equilibrium rate is traceable to the fact that the price and cost structure of the economy has moved out of line with those of major trading partners, primarily because of excessive demand and monetary creation. As explained in previous chapters of the study, the basic explanation is provided in terms of a theoretical model that assumes that the demand for money is a stable function of a discrete number of aggregate economic variables, and that the law of one price will hold in international markets, assuming no transportation costs or trade restrictions.

In this monetarist-type conceptual schema, international price and interest rate movements are linked to developments in the foreign exchange market, with the law of one price conceptualized in terms of interest rate and purchasing power parity conditions that hold at each point in time. It is in this context that exchange rate adjustment is advocated. As indicated earlier, it is predicated on the need for a realignment of the domestic price structure with that of a country's trading partners.

It must be evident that the equilibrium exchange rate, like other ideal equilibrium rates, is of limited practical significance. One reason lies in the unrealistic assumptions on which it is based. Second, it is almost impossible to compute such an exchange rate. Its determination would require the specification of complex general equilibrium models based on an integration of real and financial sectors of the economy, with a tracing of the optimal path of the exchange rate in relation to other strategic variables, such as the balance of payments. This approach cannot be meaningfully used in developing countries due to data limitations and the exogenous nature of the forces determining the behavior of most variables (Mansur 1983).

One practical policy approximation that is sometimes used in the policy analysis of the World Bank and the IMF is the "shadow" exchange rate. This is a benchmark that is considered to reflect the scarcity value of foreign exchange more adequately than the overvalued official rate. The reasoning is that the "shadow" rate reflects more adequately the opportunity cost of foreign exchange, which is the amount of domestic currency people are willing to give up in order to obtain a unit of foreign exchange.

While there are several conventions for measuring shadow foreign exchange rates, estimation is typically based on the "first best" or Pareto optimal case, which assumes optimal trade policies and the absence of market imperfections and trade distortions. In the absence of these imperfections and externalities, the optimal policy for a country that cannot affect world prices would be based on the adoption of the free trade exchange rate. It is sometimes possible to adjust this rate to take account of market imperfections and externalities. It is generally agreed, however, that while the shadow exchange rate remains an important heuristic and policy device, it nevertheless suffers from some of the same conceptual and practical limitations as other shadow or optimum rates.

Turning to more practical policy considerations, an important issue in exchange rate management concerns the relationship between the nominal and real exchange rates, and, in particular, whether a nominal devaluation of the domestic currency will increase a given economy's competitiveness by affecting the real exchange rate. In this context, the real exchange rate is considered to be an index of the real overvaluation of the currency, and substantial effort has been devoted to its measurement. The same is true of what is called the "real effective exchange rate."

In simple analytic terms, the real exchange rate represents a relative price that is equivalent to the net barter terms of trade, that is, the ratio of export prices to import prices, or the ratio of the prices of traded goods to nontraded goods. An appreciation in the real exchange rate is therefore associated with a reduction in the price of traded goods, and, given the relevant demand elasticities, by a corresponding improvement in the terms of trade. This reduces a country's export share on world markets, and increases the quantity of imports. By contrast, a decrease in the real exchange rate, or a worsening of the terms of trade results in increased competitiveness due to a fall in relative prices, an increased export share, and a reduction in imports.

A common practice in World Bank and IMF policy work is to conceptualize these relationships in terms of the nominal effective exchange rate (NEER) and the real effective exchange rate (REER). The NEER index is constructed by deflating nominal exchange rates by the corresponding indices of relative prices, as follows:

$$\text{NEER} = \Sigma \; W_{eit}, C_n, C_{tp} \hspace{3cm} 7.1$$

where W_{eit} is relevant weights (export, import, or trade shares of partner countries); C_n is the value of one unit of numeraire currency (e.g., US dollar); and C_{tp} is the value of one unit of trading partner currency in terms of the numeraire currency.

The REER is obtained by further deflating the NEER by a weighted relative price index. An aggregate weighted index is then obtained, which measures the average change in the domestic country's exchange rate vis-à-vis that of its principal trading partners.

REER = NEER/WRP

and

$$WRP = \Sigma \, W(P_d/P_f)$$

where W is the relevant weights for trading partners; P_d is relevant price index for the domestic economy; and P_f is the relevant price index for partner countries.

It is evident that there must be several statistical and methodological problems surrounding the computation and interpretation of such weights. These include, among other things, the choice of an appropriate base period, the weights to be used (exports, imports, or total trade), the domestic and foreign price indices to be used (wholesale prices, consumer prices, unit labor costs), as well as the relevant trading countries, for example, bilateral trading partners as compared to other countries that compete with the host country (Rhomberg 1976; Maciejewski 1983).

Despite these technical problems, REER measures do provide some useful information about the behavior of exchange rates. When the real effective exchange rate of a country appreciates, it implies that the country in question is suffering a loss of international competitiveness. This is normally reflected in a reduction in export earnings and an increase in import expenditures, resulting in a deterioration in the overall trade balance, and causing balance-of-payments difficulties.

One conclusion is that if a country's exchange rate policy is based solely on changes in nominal rates, it can prove inadequate in terms of the size of the nominal devaluation and other macroeconomic adjustments that are called for. The situation may be illustrated by considering the experience of some African countries that have been pursuing a relatively active exchange rate policy, but where quite large nominal devaluations have been accompanied by the appreciation or slight devaluation in the real effective exchange rate.

The IMF (1982) estimated that real effective exchange rates for currencies of African countries appreciated, on average, by about 44 percent during the 1973–81 period. Between 1980 and 1983, no less than 25 sub-Saharan African countries depreciated their nominal exchange rates. As the data in Table 7.1 show, only 16 of these managed to devalue their real effective exchange rates, and for the larger majority, the real depreciation was less than 20 percent. There was a real appreciation of the exchange rate in another 16 countries, and in nine of these the appreciation was 20 percent or above. In these countries, the relatively high rates of domestic inflation were only partially offset by exchange rate changes.

Table 7.1 *Real effective exchange rate changes in selected African countries, 1980–83*

Country	Pencentage change 1980–83
Exchange rate appreciation Niger(2), Zambia(3), Somalia(6), Zimbabwe(14)	0–20
Ethiopia(20), Chad(22), Liberia(27), Nigeria(38), Sierra Leone(53), Tanzania(77)	20 and above
Exchange rate depreciation Cameroon(-2), Senegal(-9), Sudan(-6), Kenya(-11), Burkina Faso*(-14)	0–20
Ivory Coast(-20), Zaire(-20), Benin(-24), Ghana(-37), Uganda(-78)	20 and above

Source: Data provided by the IMF Research Department (1984); and World Bank (1984a).

Note: The figures in parentheses represent changes in the real effective exchange rate. A minus sign indicates exchange rate depreciation.

*Formerly Upper Volta.

ALTERNATIVE APPROACHES TO DEVALUATION

In the evolution of orthodox economic thought on exchange rate depreciation, three more or less complementary approaches have gained wide currency, and at different times: the "Elasticities," "Absorption," and "Monetarist." As is well known, the oldest is the elasticities approach to the balance of trade. This approach views the effects of exchange rate changes primarily in terms of alterations in the relative prices of traded and nontraded goods. It was later overtaken by the Keynesian income-absorption approach which, as indicated in Chapter 3, views balance-of-payments deficits as being caused by the incompatibility between a given economy's productive capacity and its income and spending. Its overall emphasis is therefore on corrective monetary, fiscal, and exchange rate action as a means of bringing about a sustainable equilibrium between domestic absorption and output. The assumption is that, given high enough elasticities, and taking into account the relevant price and income effects, a downward adjustment of the exchange rate would result in a decline in aggregate expenditure relative to income and output, with an ultimate improvement in the balance of trade.

Exchange rate adjustment based on the elasticities and absorption approaches implicitly takes the current production, cost, and price structure as given. The price effects of a devaluation are expected to effect an overall shift in resource allocation by inducing an increased supply of exports, a reduction in import demand, and an increase in the domestic production of import substitutes. One overriding assumption is the existence of a relatively free and efficient market in which price signals reallocate resources to their more productive uses, while restraining import demand. In addition, the use of appropriate monetary and fiscal measures would then insure that income increases are kept below that of aggregate output, thereby releasing real resources for exports.

It was soon recognized that both the elasticities and absorption approaches dealt only with the balance of trade, and not with the balance of payments as a whole. The entire balance of payments has to be brought into consideration in order to determine the mechanisms through which devaluation induces a reduction in aggregate demand or domestic absorption relative to domestic production and income. Such a mechanism is suggested in various versions of the monetary approach to exchange rate adjustment (Frenkel and Johnson 1977; Dornbusch 1980; IMF 1977).

The general monetary approach assumes that: (1) people at home (the devaluing country) or abroad have access to either goods or money balances, and that the demand for money balances is positively related to income; and (2) changes in the money supply are relatively infrequent. The implication is that any increase or decrease in the money supply will be reflected in a corresponding surplus or deficit in the balance of trade. Given these assumptions, and further assuming external equilibrium conditions, a devaluation of the domestic currency is first expected to produce an increase in the domestic price level, due to increases in the local prices of traded and some nontraded goods.

This follows from assumptions underlying the law of one price due to the influence of substitution effects and/or changes in expectations. The underlying rationale is as follows: given initial demand and production conditions as well as some equilibrium price between traded and nontraded goods, a change in the exchange rate will tend to produce a shift in demand toward nontraded or home goods which are now relatively cheaper, and a shift in supply to traded goods which are now relatively more expensive. This ultimately results in an excess demand for nontraded goods, and a consequent increase in their price.

Alternatively, the increase in the price of nontraded goods may take place spontaneously through the influence produced by buyers' expectations. This is based on the assumption that they are fully aware or have some implicit notion of the equilibrium relationship between the prices of traded versus nontraded goods. Under the circumstances, a change in the price of traded goods will cause economic agents to revise their expectations about the equilibrium price of nontraded goods.

The combined effect of the domestic price increases of traded and nontraded goods will be a decline in the real value of the money balances held by the population of the devaluing country. This, in turn, is likely to produce increased hoarding in an effort to restore the real value of the money balances that the population desires to hold. This would call for an increase in savings or a reduction in aggregate expenditure, with the overall result being the creation of an excess demand for money, or the opposite: an excess supply of real goods. Over time, this will increase the availability of traded goods for export, and reduce the supply and consumption of non-traded or home goods.

The exact opposite is assumed to take place in the rest of the world. Since foreigners now experience a reduction in the price of goods imported from the devaluing country, the real value of their money balances increases, causing them to stop hoarding and increase their expenditures, relative to income, on imported goods. The overall result for the devaluing country is a balance-of-payments surplus, and for the rest of the world a balance-of-payments deficit.

In summary, the general monetarist approach analyzes the effects of exchange rate adjustment in terms of changes in the real value of money, expenditure patterns on real goods, and therefore aggregate demand. When a country devalues, domestic prices tend to rise, and prices in the external world tend to fall, with each percentage change in prices assumed to be less than the percentage devaluation of the currency. First, the real value of money balances will be reduced in the devaluing country and increased in foreign countries. Second, this will induce a reduction of expenditures on goods in the devaluing country as well as a corresponding increase in such expenditures in foreign countries. This expected result follows from the assumption that the relevant economic agents will attempt to restore the real value of their money balances, thereby generating a balance-of-payments surplus in the domestic country and a corresponding deficit in foreign ones.

ANTI-DEVALUATION

We now turn our attention to some of the criticisms that have been advanced against the devaluation policy measure, especially when it is accompanied by contractionary monetary and fiscal policies. Some of the criticisms are based on a questioning of the assumptions underlying devaluation models, while others are more concerned with the systematic effects of devaluation on relevant macroeconomic objectives such as output growth, balance-of-payments equilibrium, inflation, and employment.

First, it has been argued that the usefulness of exchange rate policy largely depends on a country's economic structure, specifically, on the degree of elasticity and diversification of the economy. Exchange rate adjustments tend to be more effective as instruments when trade flows are more responsive to price factors, particularly in those industrial nations with a highly diversified export and import structure and developing countries with a reasonably well-developed manufacturing sector. In the more industrialized nations, goods manufactured at home compete with imports and other commodities produced by trading partners, resources move relatively freely in markets, and the existing cost structure is relatively stable, since there are usually no sudden changes in productivity. By contrast, there are usually no close domestic substitutes for imports in developing countries. Further, since they mainly export a few primary commodities and relatively unsophisticated manufactured products, there is little or no relationship between the competitiveness of their exports and the cost structures of their trading partners (Nashashibi 1983).

This point is emphasized since it is typically assumed that payments deficits in developing countries reflect the fact that export prices have become less competitive in relation to import prices. The devaluation policy measure is expected to bring about changes in the relative price and cost structure, leading to an expansion in the now more competitive export sector, and a corresponding reduction in import competitiveness. The assumptions underlying the above pattern of reasoning would seem to be highly unrealistic when the true nature of the export and import structure of the majority of developing countries is taken into consideration.

On the export side, the argument is that balance-of-payments deficits are usually a reflection of a lack of flexibility in the structure of production and trade, the influence of exogenous factors, and, in some cases, the pursuit of growth and development objectives that are out of line with a country's export earning potential. To the extent that rigidities exist in the trade and production structure of developing countries, they typically reflect a lack of potentially large exportable surpluses. As a result, the decrease in export prices (in terms of foreign currency) that normally accompanies devaluation, is not likely to bring about any significant expansion in exports.

On the import side, the related argument is that there is very little price responsiveness in import demand for private consumption goods, with the exception, perhaps, of basic food items. The same is true of intermediate and capital goods, which are used in the domestic production of exportables and which usually pose a major constraint to output growth. Under such circumstances, demand management and exchange rate policies designed to reduce import demand and reallocate resources can prove to be counterproductive, unless they are combined with other policies that provide price incentives for export expansion and for removing supply bottlenecks.

On this score, a possible IMF response would be based on the contention that many of the existing bottlenecks are policy induced; that is, they have been caused by exchange controls and quantitative restrictions on trade. The evidence provided in the previous chapter would seem to lend some measure of support to such a viewpoint. In other words, one possible reason why export and import structures of developing countries do not readily adjust to changes in relative prices may be precisely because some of the structural bottlenecks are policy induced. However, as pointed out in the next chapter, there are some other important influences at work. The general conclusion that seems to emerge at this stage is that exchange rate adjustments aimed at rectifying balance-of-payments disequilibria should also be used as instruments of structural adjustment and change. It must remain an open question whether traditional exchange rate policies can meaningfully achieve this objective, and to the extent that it is achievable, whether the requisite structural changes (usually market oriented) would be related to the long-term goals of the developing countries involved.

However, to the extent that the above argument is sound, exchange rate changes needed to secure balance-of-payments equilibrium and structural change will, by necessity, have to be large. This is particularly true if nominal devaluations are to have any meaningful effect on the desired behavior of the real effective exchange rate. The time dimension of exchange rate adjustment will also have to be taken into account. It is now recognized that it takes time to change the basic structural parameters of an economy. The experience of the 1970s has certainly demonstrated that fatal political shocks and other events producing adverse consequences for the long-term growth potential are likely to ensue, if the time dimension underlying the movement toward exchange rate "equilibrium" is too compressed. To the extent that trade and exchange liberalization are considered desirable goals of development policy, a number of years are required for changes in the exchange rates to induce shifts in the requisite production and consumption structures of the developing countries.

As indicated earlier, nominal exchange rate adjustments have sometimes been accompanied by an appreciation or slight devaluation of the real effective exchange rate. This suggests that relatively small nominal devaluation do not necessarily force policy makers to take other actions that will help to develop an appropriate structure of domestic prices. A similar issue arises in terms of large discrete devaluations designed to ensure appropriate real effective rate adjustments. This undoubtedly poses a difficult political choice for the authorities in a devaluing country. The general consensus is that for a devaluation to be effective, it must not only be large enough, but must also be accompanied by accommodating types of macroeconomic policy. This is because of the short-term inflationary and cost effects of a devaluation, as well as the longer period of time required to effect appropriate structural adjustments in the economy.

Related to this is the much larger question concerning the potentially negative repercussions on domestic development goals that may accompany exchange rate adjustment, as well as the constraints that may be imposed on the ability of national authorities to undertake supportive aggregate demand and supply management policies. For example, if exchange rate adjustment is targeted toward reducing the inflation rate, the reasoning is that the government must simultaneously restrain public expenditure and relax trade restrictions, if adverse effects on the general price level are not to develop. The necessity to keep a lid on public expenditures follows from the basic philosophy underlying IMF-type programs, which posits that permanent increases in the general price level require increases in the money supply, and government budget deficit spending is the main source of such increases.

One of the most widely debated issues in both academic and policy circles concerns the potentially inflationary effects of devaluation. At one level, this can be interpreted from the perspective of the age-old debate between monetarists and structuralists. While a discussion of the finer points of that debate would take us too far afield, the bone of contention is well known. On the one hand, monetarists generally argue that inflation is basically caused by excess demand stemming from too much monetary expansion. By contrast, structuralists argue that inflation is caused by deepseated structural and supply rigidities in the economy. According to Killick and others (1982), these include a rigid agricultural and food situation, feudal agrarian structures (especially in Latin America), weak tax systems, and powerful corporatist governments as well as trade unions. Where these conditions are present, monetary restrictions and devaluation would tend to aggravate inflation and unemployment, and force an overall contraction in the economy (on this, see Findlay 1973).

The reasoning is based on the relative price and trade effects of a devaluation. First, a devaluation is supposed to change relative prices and shift the production structure in favor of the traded goods sector relative to sectors producing nontraded or domestic goods. It therefore raises the relative domestic price of traded goods. To the extent that such traded goods form an important component in workers' budgets, devaluation will therefore reduce their consumption, forcing a reduction in real wages. If workers are well organized, this is likely to heighten demands for higher money wages, creating a spiral of higher prices in the domestic goods market, further wage demands, and so on. If this occurs, any nominal devaluation of the exchange rate may result in a rise in the prices of domestic or nontraded goods, thereby reducing the effective rate of devaluation.

Second, changes in relative prices are likely to have effects on both the balance of trade and employment. As stated earlier, devaluation is expected to reduce the domestic consumption of traded versus nontraded or domestic goods, and shift the production structure in the former direction. However, while the consumption effects can be expected to be more or less immediate in their impact, the production effects may take longer to materialize because of the structural and institutional rigidities mentioned earlier. Thus, while the short-run effect of a devaluation may be some improvement in the balance of payments, the overall impact is very likely to be a contraction of economic activity and employment. This would seem to be a more likely possibility since devaluation is normally accompanied by monetary contraction. The above points are well developed in Krugman and Taylor (1978).

A third possibility is that producers may take the opportunity of capitalizing on the publicity that usually accompanies a devaluation, by raising output prices. This is especially likely in those cases where the devaluation involves a large discrete change in exchange rates. As Cooper reminded us some years ago, a large discrete devaluation can serve as an excuse to producers to raise the prices of certain products where it was difficult to do before the exchange rate change "for reasons of law, custom, fear of public opprobrium or simple inertia" (1971, p. 27). It is also possible that frequent changes in the exchange rate, irrespective of the size of the adjustment, may result in expectations that such changes will continue to move in the same direction, thereby furthering inflationary pressures.

Some analysts also point to the potentially adverse effects of devaluation on real income distribution. One line of argument is that devaluation, in general, tends to increase the real incomes of entrepreneurs in export and import competing sectors, while decreasing the real incomes of other population groups, including farmers who do not produce for the export market, and who may be in need of fertilizers and other imported inputs. From another perspective, it tends to shift the income distribution in favor of owners of capital and against wage earners. As emphasized by Cline (1983), on the assumption that most savings are derived from profits and not from wages, the result is likely to be a shift in the income distribution in the direction of increased profits and savings, and a concomitant squeezing in consumption and living standards of the working class.

The argument that devaluation, by shifting the income distribution from wages to profits, may provide a potential stimulus to savings, can be questioned on several grounds. First, it implicitly assumes that the marginal propensity of capitalists to save is higher than that of wage earners (see the arguments in Chapter 4, pp. 50–51). It may be commented that there can be no presumption that the marginal propensity of profit earners to save is necessarily higher than that of wage earners. Further, since the success of a devaluation is usually predicated on the increased profitability of the traded goods sector, the more intensive use of labor and raw materials becomes a critical factor. This assumes that the drive to improve the profitability of the traded goods sector will not be accompanied by use of a more capital-intensive and labor-displacing technology, but by a more rational and skillful use of the country's resource endowments, including labor.

Finally, besides the dubious price and allocation effects of devaluation, mention must be made of the potentially negative social, distributional, and developmental costs associated with this measure. First, in cases where the devaluing country is heavily dependent on imports of food and consumption goods, the increased price of these goods that accompanies devaluation may result in significant hardships for certain social groups. This may be considered an undesirable result where wage and incentive goods are needed for the more productive segments of the population, especially if they lack political power. Second, to the extent that devaluation raises the prices of intermediate and capital goods, this will be translated into higher production costs, a possible reduction in the price competitiveness of exports, and economic malaise.

PART IV

EVALUATION AND RESPONSES: SOME FURTHER QUESTIONS

8

The Burden of Adjustment

One of the most difficult problems posed for stabilization and adjustment programs concerns the relative degree of emphasis to be given to external versus internal factors in the interpretation of the imbalances facing the developing countries. In this context, one important question is whether balance-of-payments deficits are caused not so much by internal demand management factors, but more by structural characteristics that define the operation of the global political economy.

Some analysts argue that these imbalances are traceable, in the main, to the operation of global forces beyond the control and influence of the developing countries. This is not to deny that many of these countries may not have compounded these difficulties by the types of development policies they were willing to pursue. To the extent that any credence can be lent to the argument based on global forces, it becomes reasonable to suggest that these imbalances tend to be worsened by the adjustment policies proposed under IMF stabilization programs. This is because the burden of adjustment might have been shifted to the developing countries themselves, with insufficient attention being paid to the influence of exogenous factors.

This chapter highlights some of the more well-known exogenous factors and juxtaposes them against some of the more important internal factors that affect the adjustment process. While the analysis poses difficult questions of causal empiricism, a fundamental question is whether the direction of causation is from internal demand mismanagement to external deficits, and not the other way around. A related question is whether the capacity to adjust, at least in the short run, is not severely constrained by the nature of the structural and supply rigidities facing developing countries.

While meaningful empirical analysis can help to throw light on these questions, the answers must ultimately depend on the paradigm of development one supports. For example, supporters of the more heterodox world view schematized in Table 8.1 would argue that, in the discussion of adjustment problems, more emphasis should be put on the concentration of external reliances, and the relevant consequences for the internal growth and development process carefully analyzed. An illustration of these external reliances and their internal consequences is provided in Table 8.2. A few of the more specific factors defining the external environment are highlighted below.

Table 8.1 *Heterodox perspectives of economic development*

Analysis and method	*Models and theories*	*Goals and values*
Normative	Neo-structuralism	Human development
Contextualism	Neo-institutionalism	Growth with equity
Interdisciplinary	Dependency	Basic human needs
Systems	Balanced growth	fulfillment
Disequilibrium		
Development processes	*Global structure*	*Policy thrust*
Organic	Asymmetrical	Broad-based development
Structural change	Stratified	Unified development
Institutional change	Imperfect markets	National developmentalism
Local resource use		Activist role for state
Auto-centered		Decentralized planning

Source: Compiled by author.

THE EXTERNAL ENVIRONMENT

First, as the data in Table 8.3 indicate, the current account deficits, especially of non–oil-developing countries, have now reached unprecedented proportions. Recession in the developed countries has reduced the export earnings of their developing counterparts, while high real interest rates increased their debt service obligations. According to Dell and Lawrence (1980), these deficits should therefore be interpreted in terms of their relationship to the "structural surpluses" earned by the major industrial as well as OPEC nations.

The argument is that, since the days of the 1973–74 oil crisis and the various world recessions and periods of slow growth that ensued, the major industrial countries have been able to shift the burden of adjustment to the developing countries. The explanation is provided by the following factors: the general shift toward monetary restraint in the major industrial countries, as evidenced by the upsurge of interest rates; the slackening of the pace of import demand in these countries; on a related basis, the general

Table 8.2 *External reliances and internal consequences*

Reliances and consequences	Characteristics
External reliances	
Trade	High proportion of trade in GNP.
Commodity trade concentration	High percentage share in total exports and GNP of two to three most important commodity exports.
Trade partner concentration	Relatively high proportion of trade with one country or region.
Vertical trade disposition	High proportion of unprocessed to processed exports, with high ratio of processed goods in total imports.
Export earning instability	Wide year-to-year fluctuations in export prices and earnings.
Technological	All technologically sophisticated products and processes have to be imported.
Food imports	Historical changes in net food and grain trade, with increasing proportion of basic food items imported.
Financial	High proportion of capital imports in domestic capital formation, and high external public debt.
Internal consequences	
External control	High percentage of external control of production.
Sectoral disarticulation	Uneven development across sectors and regions.
Monocultural attachment	High proportion of labor force in traditional sectors.
Export crop concentration	Neglect of food subsector and rural production.
Low incomes	Low and stagnating GNP per capita.

Source: Compiled by author.

Table 8.3   *Balance of payments of developing countries, 1970–82*

	1970	1980	1981	1982
Current account balance	-12.0	-58.9	-118.5	-118.3
Financed by net capital inflows	12.7	81.6	96.6	85.2
Official	5.8	34.2	33.3	34.9
Private loans	4.7	35.3	47.7	35.0
Direct private investment	2.2	12.1	15.6	15.3
Use of reserves	-0.7	-22.8	22.0	33.0

Figures in billions of current dollars.
Source: World Bank data tapes; and World Bank 1983.

undermining of the buoyancy of export markets for primary commodities, not only in terms of export volumes, but more importantly in terms of severe weaknesses of export prices; and simultaneously, a continued up-surge in the import prices facing developing countries, with adverse conse-quences for inflation rates and their terms of trade.

The rise in import prices and the corresponding fall in export prices have tended to undermine attempts by many governments to improve their balance of payments and practice sound economic mangement. In develop-ing countries, major programs designed to improve the structure of agricultural and industrial incentives have been upset by the desperate shortage of foreign exchange. This has resulted from drastic and persistent falls in the export prices of certain primary commodities. The situation has also been aggravated by rising debt service commitments. In other coun-tries, the increase in incentive prices paid to producers of major crops was followed by a significant fall in world market prices. Consequently, efforts aimed at restoring balance of payments and budgetary equilibria had to be abandoned.

Further, according to projections made by the World Bank's com-modity department, the deterioration in export prices is unlikely to show any significant reversal during the next decade. A sizable fall in the real prices of coffee, cocoa, and tea is envisaged, compared to the average levels recorded over the past 20 years. The same is true for a large number of other commodities. As an example, while mineral products can be expected to recover from the extremely low price levels of recent years, the projections show that they would remain far below the average levels attained during the 1960s.

Other factors contributing to this gloomy picture about the interna-tional environment include the traditionally high commodity and partner concentration of trade, and the wide fluctuations in export earnings, which continue to be the lot of developing countries. The evidence suggests that such commodity price fluctuations are caused mainly by the volatility of export prices. In general, the short-run demand and supply elasticities of the major commodities exported by the developing countries tend to be low, resulting in year-to-year fluctuations in prices, and therefore export revenues. Further, while there is no consensus about the incidence of export earnings instability, the available empirical evidence generally supports the hypothesis that both the commodity and partner concentration of trade tend to be positively correlated with export earnings instability. Such export instability tends to have negative consequences not only for growth, investment, and import capacity, but more importantly, for the overall capacity of developing countries to manage their economies in a meaningful sense.

The factors that are primarily responsible for such export earnings instability are well known. For some commodities, the influence operates mainly from the demand side, with the relevant price fluctuations traceable to changes in overall economic activity in the industrial countries, which are, by and large, the primary purchasers of commodities in the world market. In other cases, supply factors tend to be more important: output fluctuations brought about by changes in weather, temperature, and other environmental factors.

The export potential of developing countries continues to be eroded by protectionism in the industrial nations. While the specific modality of protectionism may vary from commodity to commodity, or from country to country, virtually all developed nations protect their agriculture and industry to some extent. As mentioned in an earlier part of the study, the trade restrictions imposed by developed countries include both tariffs and nontariff barriers, and these very in severity among countries and products. These restrictions tend to lower world prices and restrict the volume of exports from both the developed and the developing world. Further, the restrictions tend to escalate in relation to the degree of processing, that is, as goods are developed from raw materials to semi-processed products to a finished state. Developing countries are therefore discouraged from the local processing of raw materials designed for the export market.

One specific area of concern continues to be the nature of agricultural protectionism, and its implications for the balance of payments of developing countries. In most industrial nations, high domestic price supports for agricultural products have often encouraged domestic production that cannot be absorbed at prevailing prices. The result is a disposal of stocks in international markets, with a consequent displacement of more efficient developing country producers.

It is now generally believed that the national protectionist policies of the major industrial nations tend to promote domestic political objectives at the expense of increased international trade and imports from the developing world. In general, agricultural protection in the developed nations has resulted in overproduction and underconsumption of agricultural output in these countries, as well as distortions in the allocation of resources between agriculture and other sectors. As pointed out by IMF staff analysts and others, large exportable surpluses have developed, and these have been disposed of in international markets through export subsidization, thereby imposing costs on taxpayers or consumers in the protecting countries, as well as on more efficient producers abroad (Anjaria et al. 1982).

The potential expansion of world trade that is likely to accompany increased trade liberalization by the developed world will therefore produce significant welfare gains for developing countries, through increased market access and the related possibilities offered for the expansion of export earnings. For example, a study conducted by analysts at the International Food Policy Research Institute (IFPRI) on the effects of agricultural protection on the developing world shows that a hypothetical 50 percent across-the-board reduction in tariffs and other barriers for 90 commodities in 17 developed OECD countries would result in an expansion of world trade by about $8.5 billion per year (Valdés and Zietz 1980).

The study shows that developing countries are likely to capture between 50 and 80 percent of the increase in world trade that is likely to result from liberalization. The commodities that would be most affected include raw and refined sugar, beef and veal, green coffee, wine, tobacco, and maize. When the commodities are grouped into categories used in GATT negotiations, sugar, sugar derivatives, and meats are expected to capture nearly 50 percent of the increase in export revenues expected by developing countries.

Liberalizing the international trade in sugar would therefore bring substantial benefits to developing country producers. International trade in sugar represents about one-third of world production, with developing countries accounting for about 65 percent of world trade. Historically, international trade has been governed by the International Sugar Agreement. However, in more recent times, this mechanism has proved inadequate to deal with the cyclical changes in the world market. The ACP countries sell certain quantities of sugar to the European Economic Community (EEC) at prices guaranteed under the Lome Convention. However, the highly subsidized production of sugar in the European Community has resulted in production levels averaging 25 percent or more in excess of its consumption requirements. This has increased the Community's export surplus, which is then dumped on the international market through export subsidies.

The EEC has therefore increased its share of world sugar exports, with traditional sugar exporters complaining vehemently, under the provisions of the GATT, about the EEC's sugar export policy. The EEC has attempted to meet these complaints by substituting producer-financed export subsidies for subsidies financed through its own budget. However, the overall implications for major sugar importers, including those from the developing world, have not changed.

The other major sugar importing country is the United States, where domestic production and imports of sugar have for a long time been regulated through a succession of sugar acts. As in the case of other national sugar policies, these measures have had both economic and political significance. They were essentially designed to provide a remunerative and stable income to domestic producers through direct government subsidies. These domestic price support levels have been traditionally high. In order to avoid the budgetary cost of maintaining support levels in the face of falling world sugar prices, the United States in 1982 raised its sugar import fee and imposed country-specific quotas on sugar imports.

The Debt Crisis

Finally, mention must be made of the deepening of the financial reliances that have accompanied the skyrocketing balance-of-payments deficits of developing nations. This increasing financial dependency reflects the cumulative interplay of both external and internal factors, with the external factors predominating. These are in part a reflection of the externally propelled development path followed by the larger majority of developing nations. As indicated in Chapter 4, the internal variables reflect the institutional maladjustments and inefficiencies associated with the domestic process of financial mobilization and intermediation.

One of the more enduring external factors continues to be the burden produced by increased, and at times excessive, external borrowing. As the data in Table 8.4 show, the total debt outstanding and disbursed to the developing countries was around $596 billion in 1983 compared to $68 billion in 1970.

Table 8.4 *Debt profiles of developing countries, 1970–83*

Ratios	1970	1974	1980	1982	1983
Total debt (outstanding and disbursed)[a]	68.4	141.0	424.8	538.0	595.8
Official	33.5	61.2	157.5	190.9	208.5
Private	34.9	79.8	267.3	347.1	387.3
Ratios (as percentages)					
Of debt to GNP	13.3	14.0	19.2	24.9	26.7
Of debt to exports	99.4	63.7	76.1	108.7	121.4
Of interest service to GNP	0.5	0.7	1.5	2.2	2.2
Debt service ratio[b]	13.5	9.5	13.6	19.9	20.7

Source: World Bank Debt Reporting Service; and World Bank 1984.
[a]In billions of current dollars.
[b]Ratio of interest payments plus amortization to exports.

This has been accompanied by an increase in the debt burden, and a corresponding deterioration in credit-worthiness. Between 1970 and 1982, ratios of debt to GNP had risen from 13 to 27 percent, of debt to exports from 99 to 121 percent, and of debt service (interest and amortization payments) to exports from 13 to 21 percent.

Besides the sheer magnitude of increase in both the absolute debt and the debt burden, there has been an equally dramatic shift in the composition of the debt as well as in its maturity structure. This is explained by the increasing proportion of the debt that is owed to private creditors. In 1970, private commercial institutions held about 12 percent of this debt, but by 1980, the proportion had increased to over 40 percent. By the end of 1982, the long-term debt owed to banks and other private creditors comprised approximately half the total, while the proportion of short-term debt (nearly all owed to private creditors) had risen to nearly 19 percent. The increase in the share of the short-term component would have been appreciably larger, had it not been for rescheduling arrangements negotiated by some of the major borrowers (IMF 1983).

Associated with increased private and commercial lending has been the progressive concentration of borrowing in obligations in which interest rates are adjusted at frequent intervals to rates prevailing in international money markets. The lion's share of commercial lending has taken the form of syndicated bank loans with floating interest rates. These floating or variable interest rates are usually expressed as a margin above the London Interbank Offered Rate (LIBOR). The burden of these variable interest rates lies in the incremental interest charges, which have to be borne by the majority of developing countries. To illustrate, the 33 largest developing country borrowers had a total variable interest rate debt of around $180 billion at the beginning of 1980. For each percentage point increase in LIBOR, these countries faced an extra interest charge of about $1.8 billion a year.

Needless to say, there has also been an uneven geographical distribution of the debt. At the end of 1982, 20 major borrowers accounted for 73 percent of the debt owed by non–oil-exporting developing countries, and for over 88 percent of the short-term debt (Table 8.5). While very poor countries do not borrow excessively from private market sources, their long-term official borrowing tends to be quite large in relation to their debt servicing capacity. A good illustration is provided by the situation facing low-income African countries. The outstanding medium and long-term debt of these countries amounted to only $22.6 billion in 1983, indicating a relatively low level of overall indebtedness. However, many of these countries have been unable to service their debt, resulting in a large number of reschedulings. According to the World Bank (1984), nearly half of the reschedulings that took place between 1975 and 1983 were by African countries, with Zaire alone accounting for six, Togo five, and Liberia four.

Table 8.5 *Distribution of outstanding debt among selected country groups, 1982*

Debt	Major borrowers[a] Amount	%	Low income[b] Amount	%	Others[c] Amount	%
Total debt	447.0	73.0	56.6	9.2	108.8	17.8
Short-term debt	99.7	88.4	3.0	2.7	10.0	8.9
Long-term debt	347.3	69.5	53.6	10.7	98.8	19.8
Official creditors	93.7	48.5	44.8	23.2	54.7	28.3
Private creditors	253.6	82.7	8.8	2.9	44.1	14.4

Source: Based on World Bank and Bank for International Settlements data.
Amounts in billions of dollars.

[a]The 20 countries in the non–oil developing group with the largest estimated debt to private creditors are: Mexico, Brazil, Argentina, Chile, Peru, Ecuador, Colombia, Korea, Philippines, Thailand, Malaysia, Greece, Morocco, Egypt, Yugoslavia, Israel, Turkey, Portugal, Romania, and Hungary.
[b]Excluding India and China.
[c]Residual group of countries, including India and China.

The sheer magnitude of debt increases, combined with the changes in the debt structure and the debt burden that have taken place during a period of exceptionally high interest rates, have contributed to a very serious widening of current account deficits, and therefore resulted in the increased overall financial requirements of the developing countries. For example, the combined current account deficits of oil-importing developing countries grew from $29 billion in 1978 to $82 billion in 1981, due in part to rapid increases in interest payments on their debt. In 1982, the interest due from all developing countries was about $66 billion. This constituted more than 50 percent of their total current account deficit (World Bank 1984).

In summary, the rise in external indebtedness, and the increasing significance of private creditors are a result of a constellation of forces that continue to heighten the overall dependency of the developing nations on the wider global economy. This situation does not represent a growth and maturity of global interdependence, but rather a hardening of asymmetrical relationships and the process of vertical interaction. The process has been fueled by several interdependent factors. These include: (1) the increase in foreign exchange payments for more expensive oil, petroleum-based products, and imports of food, consumption, and capital goods; (2) the relative stagnation in commodity export earnings due to the cyclical weakness of primary product prices, declines in export volumes, and a deterioration in both the commodity and income terms of trade; (3) prolonged global recessions, the weakening of demand in industrial countries, and high interest rates; and (4) a widening of the development gap.

The overall result has been a drain on already depleted foreign exchange reserves, thereby forcing the developing countries to borrow even more heavily in international capital markets. As indicated in Chapter 3, this was accompanied by an extensive use of IMF high-conditionality credits that required the compression of the balance-of-payments adjustment process over an unduly short period of time. Factors operating in the international environment, combined with internal structural rigidities, lead to the conclusion that an appropriate policy is one that lengthens the period of adjustment, with the appropriate relaxation in conditionality principles. As stated in the Brandt Commission Report:

> . . . The Fund's insistence on drastic measures, often within the time framework of only one year, has tended to impose unnecessary and unacceptable political burdens on the poorest, on occasion leading to "IMF riots" and even to the downfall of governments. . . . Many developing countries now face many pressures on their balance of payments which are outside their control. . . . The deficits for which a government can be held responsible should surely be distinguished from those that are due to short-term factors beyond its control . . . . the Fund should generally restrict detailed regulation and endeavour to place the process of adjustment (including the rate of adjustment) in the context of maintaining long-term economic and social development. . . . Because adjustments in developing countries often require more time than the Fund's relatively short-term lending facilities now provide, we suggest . . . a substantial expansion in programme lending by other international institutions. . . . If the IMF is truly to take broader domestic development objectives into account, it should also recruit and promote more people from developing countries with appropriate qualifications and sensitivity to the problems involved (1980, pp. 216–17).

INTERNAL DISEQUILIBRIA AND
THE CAPACITY TO ADJUST

Mention was made earlier of the various structural and institutional rigidities that are embedded in the fabric of developing countries, and which, by and large, define their condition of underdevelopment. In this context, the claim has been advanced that while disequilibria associated with aggregate demand management are still important, more attention should be paid to supply bottlenecks traceable to resource immobility, market fragmentation, and the disequilibria between sectoral demands and supplies. This is because these are considered to cause bottlenecks in the supply of foreign exchange and savings and intermediate inputs, as well as in the overall production structure.

As mentioned in Chapter 2, these factors are now receiving increasing attention in the policy understandings worked out between the developing countries and the IMF and World Bank. Evidence of this is the recognition of the need for an optimal mix of demand and supply management policies, and for lengthening the period of adjustment. However, there still remains disagreement in academic and policy circles about the origins of these structural rigidities, as well as the factors that may be responsible for their perpetuation.

Neo-structuralists, dependency theorists, and to some extent analyses emanating from UN agencies such as UNCTAD and ECLA seem to support a perspective of thought that views these structural rigidities as externally induced, and as a by-product of the external reliances that have accompanied the evolution of dependent capitalism in its modern forms. By contrast, the IMF/World Bank perspective, while recognizing the influence of exogenous factors or "external shocks," places much more emphasis on internal economic factors.

It is evident that, from a policy perspective, most of the external variables must remain outside the control of the developing nations, at least in the short run. This is because the removal of external constraints is intimately bound up with the success or failure of schemes for changing the present international economic order. The hardening of attitudes that has taken place over the years provides an important ground for pessimism. At the same time, developing countries would have much more to gain from continued participation in the international economic system, rather than disengaging from it or moving in the direction of increased autarkic development. This should not be interpreted to mean that appropriate forms of self-reliant development should not be encouraged. However, while the dialogue for changing the structure of international relationships continues, the nature and influence of exogenous factors will have to be taken as given.

There can be no doubt that some of the structural rigidities are of historical origin, and are inherently connected with the structure and functioning of the international economic system. However, a large number have been induced, and/or perpetuated by the developing countries themselves. As emphasized in Chapter 6, a variety of economic sectors are administered in pursuit of goals other than efficient resource allocation. In many cases, the stated goals are laudable ones, but in actuality reflect the pursuit of private or group interests of a rent-seeking nature.

Further, the policy instruments used by most governments in developing countries include various forms of price fixing through trade monopolies, exchange controls, quantitative restrictions on trade, as well as the usual decisions on taxes, subsidies, and investments. As a result, many price, cost, and other distortions have emerged, producing wide divergences between price incentives and social goals. Under these circumstances, the structural and institutional rigidities cannot be expected to move resources in the direction of allocative efficiency, especially in the short run.

In this context, the internal capacity to adjust is typically influenced by both economic and noneconomic factors, with the latter being predominant in a large number of cases. At the economic level, emphasis is usually placed on the limited price responsiveness of output, especially in agriculture. In this case, advocates of liberalization have emphasized the large number of adverse allocative, distributive, and growth effects that are associated with the common practice of setting the relevant prices below what is considered to be world market or competitive levels.

In the case of producer prices, the assumption is that there is a positive supply response in agriculture, that farmers are very responsive to profit, and therefore to price incentives. There is some empirical evidence which suggests that changing relative prices tends to have a positive effect on resource allocation among crops. However, the impact on aggregate output is less certain. There are a host of nonprice factors that tend to militate against the incentive effects that are supposed to accompany price increases. These include, among others, the lack of wage goods to the rural population, poor infrastructure, the mistrust of government, and the lack of technology. Further, price policies are likely to be counterproductive in a situation where the most lucrative opportunities for employment and economic advancement still remain in the urban sector.

Another factor inhibiting the capacity to adjust is perhaps the lack of fiscal flexibility in the decision-making process of most developing countries. At one level, this may be a reflection of the relatively poor state of institutional development at all levels, or the failure to build appropriate ones. More specifically, it reflects the relatively underdeveloped state of the budget management process, especially in poorer developing countries. This is exemplified by the fact that there is limited expenditure control in many cases, with expenditures tied into pet projects or to large, lumpy investments that cannot be abandoned or meaningfully controlled. Some may argue that these types of expenditures also take place in the more developed countries. Such a justification misses the point, since the relevant financial and managerial resources are more limited in the developing countries compared to their more developed counterparts.

The above factors are meant to be illustrative. However, to the extent that they represent elements of the structural and institutional rigidities facing developing countries, steps should be taken to remove them. This is an area where the "policy dialogue" usually associated with the granting of IMF and World Bank credits could be beneficially used. In any event, the ultimate responsibility rests with the national authorities in developing countries. They must first recognize the need for removing the relevant structural bottlenecks, and show a willingness to take appropriate action.

While the primary focus of this study is on economic issues, and less on the "politics" of stabilization, IMF-supported programs tend to highlight the fact that many of the inherent problems of stabilization and adjustment are political in nature. The IMF, in terms of its mandate, should not interfere in the internal political decision-making process of its members. Nevertheless, the general question still remains whether the internal capacity to adjust is not in fact highly constrained by the nature of politics.

In this context, an important factor in the adjustment process concerns who (the specific individuals or groups in society) should bear the burden and costs that are associated with this process. First, while the "politics of stabilization" is an area that calls for further research, a tentative hypothesis is that groups without much economic and political power are normally the ones most affected. The adjustment burden tends to fall inordinately on certain segments of the urban working population: lower- and middle-order public servants, teachers, policemen, and, to some extent, the urban and rural poor. By contrast, it can also be hypothesized that political and technocratic elites do not suffer major changes in their life styles as a result of IMF stabilization and adjustment programs. To the extent that this is true, programs will have to be so structured as to ensure a more uniform distribution of the relevant costs and benefits.

9

Stabilization and Adjustment versus Development

This chapter addresses in a more systematic fashion some of the broader development consequences of the IMF policy paradigm. As previously mentioned, the IMF is considered an "adjustment" rather than a "development" institution like the World Bank. This is because its stabilization programs focus primarily on restoring macroeconomic equilibrium over the short and medium term, and less on the attainment of broad development goals such as income distribution, poverty alleviation, and maximum economic participation. A related viewpoint is that the Fund is more concerned with "technical" economic matters, and has not been given the mandate to become involved in issues of a political or social nature. The reasoning is that issues relating to income distribution and poverty alleviation represent political and social priorities, and therefore are the proper concern of national political leaders.

Be that as it may, a meaningful attempt can be made to interpret the role of the IMF from a much wider developmental perspective. The need for such a line of analysis can be rationalized on several grounds. In the first place, Article 1(V) pays explicit recognition to the need for output, real income, and output growth, even though the emphasis is on the orderly expansion of these variables in a liberal and stable world environment governed by balanced international trade. Second, the policy understandings associated with Fund-supported programs usually call for far-reaching changes in the entire policy spectrum of developing countries, with more emphasis placed on desired changes in pricing and incentive structures. Third, and on a related basis, while the focus of most stabilization programs is on short- or medium-term adjustment, the conditions underlying them are usually so stringent as to have severe consequences for the longer-term development process. As such, they influence to a significant degree the capacity of borrowing member countries to formulate long-term development plans and coherent strategies.

From an overall development perspective, this chapter is concerned with three interrelated types of issues. First, while it may be difficult to identify directly the essential elements of an IMF "development philosophy," it can be taken as an article of faith that an implicit assumption underlying its approach is that steps taken to improve economic efficiency will ultimately lead to the attainment of broad-based developmental goals. In this regard, a common presumption is that policies that are generally desirable on efficiency grounds tend to be the ones that help to improve the income distribution. In addition, the claim has been made that the large majority of the poor living in rural areas tend to benefit from balance-of-payments improvement programs, because of the potentially salutary effects on the internal terms of trade between the rural sector and the rest of the economy (Finch 1983, pp. 77–78).

In this context, it may be useful to compare the philosophy implicit in the Fund's approach with that of institutions such as the World Bank and the larger United Nations system. A second set of issues is related to the broad goals of IMF stabilization programs and how these interact with national development priorities. Third, there is the more general and complex issue surrounding the relative roles of prices and markets as they relate to the government and the state in the development process.

ALTERNATIVE DEVELOPMENT PERSPECTIVES: UN, WORLD BANK, IMF

As a point of departure, it may be useful to consider the broad interpretation of development provided by the United Nations. While there are several statements of the UN approach, a useful example is provided in the preamble to the *International Development Strategy* proclaimed by the UN General Assembly on October 24, 1970. It states:

> The ultimate objective of development must be to bring about sustained improvement in the well-being of the individual and to bestow benefits on all. If undue privileges, extremes of wealth and social injustice persist, then development fails in its essential purpose. This calls for a global development strategy based on joint and concentrated action by developing and developed countries in all spheres of economic and social life; in industry and agriculture, in trade and finance, in employment and education, in health and housing, in science and technology.

Further, the broad dimensions of such an approach were articulated in the *UN General Assembly Resolution No. 2681 (XXV)* of December 11, 1970, as follows:

(a) to leave no sector of the population outside the scope of change and development;

(b) to effect structural change which favors national development and to activate all sectors of the population to participate in the development process;

(c) to aim at social equity, including the achievement of an equitable distribution of income and wealth in the nation;

(d) to give high priority to the development of the human potentials, including vocational and technical training, and the provision of employment opportunities and meeting the needs of the children.

The framework outlined above carries several implications. First, it is more concerned with some of the more fundamental or ultimate objectives of development, rather than with the more proximate or intermediate ends. The latter relate to the goals and targets through which they may be achieved, such as output and real income growth, improvements in the balance of payments, fiscal integrity, and so on. Second, to the extent that such proximate ends are necessary for the attainment of ultimate objectives, there must be consistency among them as well as between these and higher-order objectives. Third, the framework suggests that the policy measures chosen should be of a type that would guarantee the attainment of broad-based development (for a useful discussion, see Timbergen 1976).

In passing, it should be mentioned that while the UN philosophy reflects certain moral imperatives, it is rooted in a fundamental concern over the failure of the historical growth process in the majority of developing nations to promote maximum economic welfare and authentic development for the masses of the population. In this context, development is taken to mean much more than improved economic performance measured in terms of the behavior of the relevant macroeconomic aggregates, to be a process through which the living standards of the majority of the people are raised, and opportunities provided for them to develop their potential.

In other words, the philosophy focuses attention on the "content" and "quality" of GNP and related economic aggregates in relation to their levels and rates of change. In a general sense, improvements in the content and quality of the growth process are associated with, among other things: (1) adequate employment creation; (2) meeting the basic human needs of all segments of the population; (3) reduction in inequalities, for example, through a more equitable distribution of income and wealth; and, in general, (4) the provision of a better quality of life. The overall implication is a reorientation of development values in the direction of human development, and the creation of conditions necessary for the fullest realization of the human personality. Another clear implication is that development must be considered a multidimensional process involving both capacity and output expansion as well as structural and institutional change.

Many aspects of this development philosophy were reflected in World Bank lending programs during the late 1970s. In this context, it is possible to identify at least two discrete periods in the more recent evolution of World Bank lending philosophy. The first was during the McNamara era when, as in the case of the United Nations, it was recognized that the historical growth process had bypassed the majority of the population in developing countries. During this period, the available evidence suggested that the national growth rates achieved by many developing countries since the 1950s were actually higher than the comparable rates for the industrial nations during their takeoff period. In the case of some countries (e.g., Brazil, Mexico, South Korea and Taiwan), impressive aggregate growth rates were accompanied by other noticeable achievements, particularly in manufacturing and related exports of manufactured goods. However, for the majority of developing countries, the growth process seemed to have bypassed the majority of people, and in many cases, might have worsened their lot through an increased concentration of wealth and a visible deterioration in the overall quality of life.

This led to a direct concern for poverty redressal, employment creation, and the elimination of various forms of inequality. This philosophy was implemented through increased Bank lending for agriculture and rural development, health, education, water supply, and related sectors concerned with human development and basic human needs fulfillment. The Bank's own approach was a pragmatic one based on a philosophy of "growth with distribution." It was informed by the results of an impressive number of studies which concluded that high rates of growth need not have an adverse effect on equity or relative inequality (Chenery et al. 1974).

A related policy prescription was that too great a concern for "premature" redistribution may have serious adverse consequences for economic growth because of disruptions on the presumed relationship between income concentration, savings rates, and growth. A related idea was that economic growth enables countries to avoid the political explosiveness of redistributing an existing pattern of income or asset distribution. The claim was that it makes little pragmatic sense to redistribute the existing stock of the relatively low incomes in the developing countries, if nothing is done to increase the production of goods and services, or other generators of national income. Under the circumstances, a period of transition was needed to make investment in the poor and other disadvantaged groups more productive. The nature and intensity of such investments were to be based on "distributional weights" that "reveal" the preferences of policy makers and the population at large for certain patterns of income distribution, as well as the relevant tradeoffs allowable with the growth objective.

In the case of agriculture and rural development, lending was guided by a philosophy of "integrated rural development," with the objective of improving the living conditions of the "target groups"—the rural poor—through a well-coordinated set of programs and policies designed to improve their incomes and productivity. As stated in the Bank's *Rural Sector Development Paper*:

> The objectives of rural development exist beyond any particular sector. They encompass improved productivity, increased employment and thus higher incomes for target groups, as well as minimum acceptable levels of food, shelter, education, and health. A national program for rural development should include a mix of activities including projects to raise agricultural output, create new employment, improve health and education, expand communications, and improve housing (World Bank 1975, p. 3).

The "growth with redistribution" philosophy, together with its correlate the "integrated rural development" strategy, go a long way toward meeting some of the requirements of authentic and broad-based development. It is evident that efforts to redistribute income and wealth could prove counterproductive in a situation of stagnant output, so that there is always a need for strategies that provide opportunities for the disadvantaged members of society to become more productive. However, such strategies are doomed to failure unless the political and technocratic bureaucracy shows a willingness to make the necessary institutional changes, especially at the local level. The strategy therefore cannot succeed in a situation where land, land tenure arrangements, credit, marketing, and other institutional structures still continue to cater primarily to the needs of those who are more advantaged.

While the World Bank still finances projects in the "human needs" area, a radical shift seems to have taken place in its development philosophy, with more emphasis now being placed on "structural adjustment." This shift toward a more traditional developmental emphasis is explained by at least two factors. The first factor is related to the impact of external "shocks" of the 1970s on the economies of the developing countries, resulting in an increased need for short- and medium-term adjustment assistance. Another is related to the climate of international opinion, which has become increasingly conservative over the past few years. In this milieu, the Bank has been increasingly criticized for the "softness" of its approach, and the mentality of "international welfarism."

An examination of such criticisms would take us too far afield. It needs to be reiterated, however, that the shift toward structural adjustment lending, and the related policy reforms that are advocated, have brought Bank thinking much closer to that of the IMF. Another way of stating the same proposition is that IMF thinking might have moved closer to that of the World Bank's in terms of the former institution's recognition of the need for medium-term structural adjustment and supply management in the developing world.

In the case of the World Bank, one obvious conclusion is that many aspects of the development model that became popular during the McNamara years are now being de-emphasized. Nevertheless, many analysts would argue that the Bank's approach to lending still remains much more flexible compared to that of the Fund. In this context, it is sometimes forgotten that the respective mandates of each of these organizations should be distinguished, and there is always a need for each to maintain its own separate analytical and political posture. What is true, however, is that they both have as ultimate objectives the promotion of prosperity in the developing countries, even though this is to be achieved through different channels. Their respective roles should therefore remain complementary rather than competitive.

It is evident, therefore, that the IMF mandate cannot be interpreted in the much broader sense suggested by the UN and traditional World Bank developmental models. Its primary concern is still with traditional macroeconomic goals such as output growth, price stability, balance-of-payments equilibrium and fiscal integrity. Most IMF-supported programs are still based on a diagnosis of the problems of output, balance of payments, and prices in terms of short-term demand pressures stemming from inappropriate monetary, fiscal, and exchange rate policies, with the monetary factor considered central to the process of interaction. As a result, the conditionality clauses underlying the typical stabilization program usually call for monetary contraction or slow money growth through private and public sector credit ceilings, reduced government expenditure, increased taxes, and devaluation of the domestic currency. In general, these conditions are imposed across borrowing countries, with few modifications, and with very little attention, if any, paid to the specific problems of underdevelopment.

At one level of analysis, it can be said that there is no explicit theory of development underlying the IMF policy paradigm. As emphasized throughout the study, there is no one theory underlying the paradigm. The analytical foundations consist of an eclectic admixture of monetarism, Keynesian income-expenditure theory, and various new orthodoxies that call for liberalization of trade and exchange regimes. The question still remains whether many aspects of monetarism and Keynesian macroeconomics have much relevance to the problems of development. One reason is that many of the postulates were developed for more advanced and flexible economies that have a proven capacity not only to adjust to various internal and external disequilibria, but also to maintain sustainable patterns of growth and overall economic development. Further, since the requirements of short-term stabilization cannot be considered in a vacuum, what seems to be needed is an integration of the relevant aspects of demand management theory with some appropriate tenets of development theory. It can be argued that embracing supply management represents a desired move in this direction. However, others would argue that the Fund's interpretation of the working of the economic system has not changed fundamentally. From the perspective of development over the longer term, IMF programs still seem to be guided by the dominant perspective of thought, which sees the price system and competitive market laws as the major generators of stable and balanced development.

Finally, any meaningful philosophy of broad-based development would seem to require a theory of development policy based on a flexible targets-instruments approach, rather than the fixed targets-instruments approach that seems to form the basis of the IMF policy paradigm. This follows in the tradition of orthodox macroeconomic policy, which is based on the proposition that policy instruments should be assigned to targets of policy, and that, given the relevant assumptions about information and foresight, the instruments should be assigned to the targets that they are considered to affect the most. In this context, the instruments of monetary policy have been traditionally assigned to the attainment of external equilibrium, while fiscal policy tools are used to achieve internal balance.

The fixed or "pinpoint targetry" approach underlying the IMF policy paradigm is therefore based on the implicit assumption that, under normal circumstances, it is possible to trace the precise quantitative effects of particular policy measures (monetary, fiscal, exchange rate, market prices) on the targeted macroeconomic aggregates (output, inflation, balance of payments, etc.). Both the targets and instruments are also set within certain restricted time frames in accordance with the quantitative performance criteria stipulated in stand-by credits. They also reflect the outcomes of projections made from the IMF's own macroeconomic models of developing countries.

The development welfare function is a continuous one. This implies a necessity for a more flexible targets-instruments approach that continuously balances the requirements of monetary, fiscal, and exchange stability against those concerned with structural and institutional change. In addition, there is a necessity to trace the overall consequences not only for traditional macroeconomic targets such as growth, price stability, and balance of payments, but also for employment, equity, poverty alleviation, and so on. Some analytical implications of this approach are pointed out below.

A point of emphasis, however, is that the fixed targets approach, based on the usual financial projections models, tends to be highly questionable. As emphasized by Dell (1983) and Dell and Lawrence (1980), one obvious problem concerns the reliability of the data base in setting time-bound targets. Another concerns the bluntness of the related policy measures, the size of the required policy changes, their timing, and the transmission mechanisms through which the policy actions are brought to bear on the economy.

The development experience suggests that the routes of transmission cannot be precise due to the large number of discontinuities, uncertainties, and complexities underlying the development process itself. Some of these can be traced to the variety of internal structural and institutional rigidities alluded to earlier. Others are beyond the control of the developing countries, and stem, in part, from cost inflation and the balance-of-payments deficits induced by the structural surpluses of the industrial and OPEC nations. These factors, combined with demand deflation, may have compounded the problems of slow growth, balance-of-payments disequilibria, unemployment, and overall economic retrenchment, which are now the economic lot of the majority of developing nations.

Some basic changes and/or extensions of the IMF's analytic apparatus will have to be made, if the policy–theoretical framework governing its stabilization and adjustment programs is to be brought more in line with the requirements of authentic development. First, the traditional targets and instruments would have to be substantially revised or redefined. At another level, it implies that the relevant financial and macroeconomic projections that usually guide policy should be based on more dynamic, multisectoral, intertemporal, general equilibrium models. Though such models are usually difficult to build, and their usefulness may be questioned, they are well within the analytical capabilities of institutions such as the Fund and Bank. This is perhaps one area where collaborative efforts between these two agencies might prove to be beneficial.

In essence, what is being suggested is a need to extend the conventional approach to policy modeling in the direction of more consistency-type planning models, national accounting, and data collection systems. The traditional approach relies heavily on Keynesian-type national income accounting systems based on well-known relationships between the variables emphasized in Part II. Models based on this approach are highly aggregative, do not focus on the broader objectives of development, and are primarily concerned with the functional as distinct from the personal distribution of income. As such, they tell us very little about the sources from which such incomes are derived.

By contrast, a consistency-type modeling framework calls for an accounting and conceptual schema that substantially disaggregates the relevant economic aggregates and links these to income and expenditure sources. Such a procedure can be considered a prerequisite for modeling not only the traditional kinds of economic aggregates, but also those of broad-based development. In addition, it can be used for evaluating the effects of specific targets, as well as development change in general, on regions, individual economic sectors, activities across and within sectors, as well as on the institutions in society.

One useful analytical tool in this regard is the social accounting matrix (SAM), pioneered by Richard Stone of Cambridge University, and further refined by other analysts (Pyatt and Thorbecke 1976; Pyatt and Roe 1979). The conceptual framework underlying the SAM can be looked at from two interdependent angles. In general, it can be thought of as a modular planning and analytical framework that specifies for a given economy a set of interrelated subsystems and the major relationships among variables both within and between these subsystems. From a policy perspective, the framework can be designed so as to incorporate those policy instruments that can be manipulated so as to move the entire economic system or parts of it in alternative directions. The latter reflect policy choices with respect to traditional macroeconomic targets as well as others such as employment, income distribution, and basic human needs. From a narrower perspective, the SAM can be looked at as a data classification system that, for any given point in time, can provide a disaggregated view of crucial links among the requisite policy variables.

WHOSE DEVELOPMENT PRIORITIES?

A common criticism of the IMF is that the conditionalities underlying its stabilization programs tend to militate against the ability of national authorities in the developing countries to practice sound economic planning and formulate coherent strategies of broad-based development. At one level, any meaningful analysis of this claim would require a close look at the development priorities of specific countries in which Fund-supported programs have been implemented. However, some general comments can be made on this issue, based on the available evidence and the author's field experience.

In the first place, there are relatively few developing countries that can meaningfully claim (through the national polities) that they subscribe to a consistent and well-developed set of broad-based development goals, and were/are willing to utilize a coherent set of strategies for their attainment. As a generalization, what seems to have occurred in several such countries is a situation in which rhetoric, ideological posture, and lip service to broad-based development goals have tended to overshadow the technical, pragmatic, and managerial requirements of efficient development action and economic sophistication. This is not to deny that the pages of development plans are replete with desirable broad-based development objectives.

As emphasized in the previous chapter, there are many cases in which the requirements of politics seem to have taken precedence over the need for making hard economic choices. This would seem to be true not only for the capacity and willingness of governments to implement stabilization measures, but also because of the political factors that seem to be involved in the goal-setting process. In this context, the general hypothesis may be advanced that in the majority of cases the stated development priorities do not necessarily reflect national development needs, but are more a reflection of the government's support base, as defined by its popularity and major linkages it can muster in terms of patron–client networks, party loyalties, and ethnic affiliations.

However, the emphasis given to the politicization of the development process is not meant to convey a "purist" economistic view of development. Neither is it meant to convey the impression that all national authorities in developing countries are "crooked" or rent seeking. There are still some honest and far-sighted leaders left in the developing world, and there are also instances in which national authorities subscribe to a meaningful set of broad-based development goals, and show a willingness to implement them. Thus, while there may be cases where national development priorities reflect political rather than economic choices, or are otherwise out of line with the national development needs of a country, there are other cases where the right balance is noticeable.

In the former case, IMF-type programs can be expected to produce a sobering effect, and at least help the countries involved to put their economic house in order. However, the latter case may be used as a typical example of a situation in which a potential clash is likely to develop between domestic development priorities and needs and the requirements of IMF conditionality. Such a situation is also likely to arise if a given country urgently needs foreign exchange that cannot be readily obtained from other sources; is relatively poor; and lacks economic power, status, or prestige and therefore sufficient bargaining strength on the board of the IMF.

To further illustrate, let us assume for the moment that we are dealing with a country with a clearly defined set of domestic economic priorities based on perceived national development needs. Second, suppose that these priorities are predicated on the need to fulfill not only a set of traditional macroeconomic objectives (output growth, price stability, balance-of-payments equilibrium), but also nontraditional ones (employment creation, income and wealth distribution, poverty alleviation, and basic human needs). Third, assume that in terms of its own preferred goals hierarchy, the country has maintained an optimal mix, but nevertheless places a higher store on the latter, nontraditional set. This is a hypothetical case but at the same time real, since it can be used to show how a poor, small country obtaining high-conditionality IMF credits may be forced to reorder its entire set of domestic priorities.

We may first consider the usual and fundamental IMF policy prescription concerning the balance of payments. For the majority of developing countries, whether or not they belong to the ideal category mentioned above, the immediate policy concern may not be necessarily one of achieving and maintaining overall balance-of-payments equilibrium, but more with the composition of the balance of payments; or the fact that either it cannot be sustained; or that it is incompatible with other development objectives of a longer-term policy significance. For example, some countries, in terms of their own development priorities, may want to place greater emphasis on employment creation by establishing more labor-intensive industries; and/or on the need to diversify the economy through the establishment of efficient export-promoting and import-substituting industries that make a fuller use of local resources; or otherwise on developing optimal linkages with the rest of the economy. The point of emphasis is that, to the extent that employment creation and diversification of the economic base represent feasible national development priorities, they may be pursued, irrespective of what happens to the balance of payments.

The potential conflict that may arise between the need for external payments equilibria and the overall domestic development strategy can also be highlighted by considering the role of exchange rate policy. An important point, emphasized in Chapter 7, is that the short-term balance-of-payments gains that are expected to accrue from a devaluation of the exchange rate should be weighed against the potentially negative consequences for industrialization and long-term development. This may be particularly relevant in those cases where dynamism of the industrialization and overall development process require considerable quantities of imported inputs, such as intermediate and capital goods. When this occurs, countries may choose to permit overvaluation of the domestic currency until the industrialization process gathers its own momentum.

One IMF policy prescription that poses the greatest source of conflict relates to the need for promoting internal economic balance through the practice of greater fiscal and financial discipline. In the typical stabilization program, a government may be asked to cut public expenditures across the board through a set of related measures, for example, cutting subsidies on basic consumer goods, reducing social spending, holding back wages in the face of inflation, and reducing the size of public sector employment. Such measures usually have serious consequences for income distribution. This has led to the conclusion that many IMF stabilization programs are by and large implemented at the expense of the poor.

In this context, one of the most controversial measures is the reduction of subsidies on food and basic consumer items, especially since developing countries usually keep a lid on basic food prices as a means of alleviating poverty, protecting vulnerable groups, and preventing the kinds of wage and cost inflation that might result from escalating food prices. As is well known, the IMF justification for cutting food subsidies is predicated on the principle that the sale and distribution of subsidized commodities should be at prices that reflect their true market values, and that governments should move toward a system in which the appropriate price signals instruct purchasing behavior. This decision rule is also rationalized on the grounds that the subsidized commodities do not normally reach those who are most in need. However, it is well documented that efforts to remove food subsidies can prove to be politically risky. The introduction of such measures has led to massive riots in Cairo and Tunisia, to political instability in Senegal and Sri Lanka, and even to military coups, as in Liberia in 1980.

The conditions under which governments can effectively cut subsidies are not well known and need to be further researched. In general terms, however, consideration should be given to phasing the reduction of such subsidies, and/or selective targeting, as in Sri Lanka and Jamaica. The governments of both countries have been experimenting with policies of distributing food stamps which are, in principle, limited to the poorest families. However, the effectiveness of such programs still needs considerable monitoring and analysis.

The other conflict area concerns cutting expenditures on basic social services such as health, education, and nutrition programs. The justifications used for the introduction of such measures are both direct and indirect in nature. In the former case, they relate to the need for budget control and the restoration of internal fiscal balance. The more indirect justification is based on a presumed tradeoff between aggregate consumption on the one hand, and aggregate savings and investment on the other. This follows from the traditional Keynesian dichotomy in which consumption and savings are considered to be competitive. Since expenditures on basic social services are seen as a part of the aggregate consumption equation, it is thought that their reduction would provide a stimulus to savings and investment, and therefore economic growth.

However, as stated in Chapter 4, the "consumption" of basic social services in many low-income countries is not necessarily competitive with savings and investment. They are more in the nature of "investment goods" especially for certain lower- and middle-income groups who may view them as incentives toward greater productive effort. In any event, the provision of basic social services in some of these countries is already at such low and parlous levels, that any attempts to cut them further merely represent invitations to social disaster. More generally, the prescription of such expenditure cuts run counter to development strategies that place a high premium on the fulfillment of basic human needs.

Cost-cutting measures in the area of basic social services are usually combined with others aimed at raising prices for electricity, water, transportation, and other public utilities. Once again, the decision rule is based on market efficiency criteria which stipulate that prices must be made equal to real costs. While there is still no consensus among economists about the rules that should govern the pricing of public facilities, the market bias pays little attention to the true nature of public goods. The raising of public utility prices, while desirable on efficiency grounds, tends to be cost inflationary and heightens the degree of hardship that has to be borne by wage and salary earners. In many cases, these are precisely the groups whose incomes are controlled under stabilization programs.

However, one needs to be reminded that in many developing countries, especially the poorest, large segments of the population have only tenuous links with the national and international economy. These groups can be considered marginal, receive few government services or benefits, and are not significantly affected by shifts in relative prices induced by measures such as devaluation and subsidy cuts, and, in general, monetary and fiscal austerity programs. As indicated earlier, the most seriously affected groups are usually urban workers and consumers. These are the groups that are most likely to experience an immediate fall in their real purchasing power and overall standard of living. Besides having to bear the brunt of expenditure cuts and increases in the prices of basic social services and public utilities, they also suffer loss of employment and incomes from the public service contraction and income controls that accompany austerity programs.

This tends to reinforce the conclusion that IMF stabilization programs tend to have the most adverse effects on the lower-middle and middle classes in developing countries, and may actually prevent other dynamic groups from emerging. However, the former groups tend to be the most politically active, and governments in general have to rely on them not only for their continued popularity, but also for votes at election time. The upshot of the argument is that national authorities sometimes have to face the difficult choice posed by the potential tradeoff between the economic benefits of stabilization programs and the associated political risks.

Most stabilization programs are drawn up on the widespread presumption that the general administration (in terms of the size and growth of the government's recurrent budget) is inefficient. The implication is that the same or better quality of public management can be achieved with far less personnel by public service retrenchment. In many cases, however, the reduction in public service employment has not resulted in the expected increase in efficiency, but more by a loss in both the amount and quality of service received by the public service clientele. Funds for supporting services are usually reduced when the recurrent budget is tightened, and in many cases, these funds are already at levels too low for the effective operation of such services.

Expenditure on defense and internal security has increasingly become one of the most important expenditures in the recurrent government budget in developing countries. Yet stabilization programs do not pay much attention to this form of expenditure. This reflects an unfortunate bias for at least two reasons. First, and as indicated above, expenditures on subsidies and basic social services are usually subjected to critical scrutiny. They therefore become candidates for excision while the defense and security budgets are left more or less intact. Second, many would view these expenditures as economically unproductive and wasteful.

The overall conclusion that emerges at this stage is that the effectiveness of stabilization and adjustment policies should be judged from a dynamic developmental perspective. As one commentator states:

. . . stabilization policy should not be viewed as a substitute to development policy. It is often the case that constraints in development, such as foreign exchange availability or insufficient domestic saving, are perceived by international credit organizations as the targets of policy. It is not clear why a developing country should thrive to reduce the deficit in its current account or what the criteria should be for doing so. It is clear, however, that there should be a long-run steady-state path that policy should be aiming for depending on a country's level of development, but such considerations have not yet been seriously addressed by the IMF (Katseli 1983, p. 363).

PRICES, MARKETS, AND THE STATE

Liberalization and supply management policies are based, by and large, on the assumption that prices do, and ought to, play a fundamental role in the processes of allocation, distribution, growth, and development. The need to "get prices right" is now part of the conventional wisdom. This refers to the entire structure of prices for inputs, outputs, and foreign exchange. It implies a greater reliance on decentralized decisions through market mechanisms, and therefore the design of policies that place a greater emphasis on the role of the private sector.

As is well known, the standard textbook treatment of the pricing standard identifies at least three sets of principles that should govern its behavior. One is the principle of nondomination, which requires that the number of buyers and sellers in the market be sufficiently large so as to prevent market dominance by any single group or groups by means of price fixing, setting the terms of transactions, or the use of collusive devices. A second is the principle of nonseparation, which requires that the market be undifferentiated, thereby preventing the possibility of various forms of market discrimination at both national and international levels, and among different types of producers and consumers. A third requirement is that of open pricing, that production, consumption, and related decisions should be based on a free and open flow of information, as a means of guaranteeing the openness of pricing decisions.

These theoretical and normative ideals are supposed to hold at all levels, with the implication that the behavior of prices in the domestic economy should be guided by a set of international prices. The latter proposition, or what is termed here "the world price standard," is inherent in the "law of one price," the "law of one interest rate," as well as the criteria used for determining various sets of equilibrium, optimum, or shadow prices in production, trade, and exchange.

We begin by considering some of the methodological and related difficulties posed by this approach. The emphasis is on the criteria used for determining the optimum sets of prices in agriculture and trade policy, though some other cases are also identified. The discussion should be considered an extension of that begun in Parts II and III.

World Price Fundamentalism Revisited

A general issue revolves around the use of a set of world prices as benchmarks for determining appropriate domestic pricing policies and liberalization strategies. As a general proposition, while the world price standard may be useful in determining practical approximations to a set of "efficiency" or "accounting" prices, and can therefore serve as a guide to policy, there are several reasons why it cannot be used indiscriminately.

World prices are supposed to reflect the opportunity cost of traded inputs and outputs. However, most of these prices are not determined in open and free markets in which the principles of nondomination, nonseparation, and open pricing can be presumed to hold. There are more reflective of the oligopolistic control of world markets by dominant industrial countries and/or transnational corporations.

Another problem, alluded to elsewhere, is the wide fluctuations experienced in the world market prices of commodities that are internationally traded. Such fluctuations are particularly harmful to the agricultural sector. One of the problems for this sector concerns the time lags that occur between changes in world prices and adjustments in domestic production. In many cases, such production reactions tend to accentuate rather than offset fluctuations in supply and prices. Further, the evidence suggests that the accompanying uncertainties tend to produce depressing effects on agricultural investment and production, especially among subsistence farmers.

Evidence of such uncertainties can also be found in the system of generalized floating of exchange rates, which came into effect with the major currency realignments in 1973. This poses a dilemma for the kind of exchange rate policy that developing countries can meaningfully follow. First, adherence to the world price standard implies that exchange rate policies should be based on criteria such as openness and flexibility, and that the currencies of developing countries will have to float in international markets. However, as Bautista (1980) points out, the pursuit of such a policy will provide no basis for demand and use of the currencies of developing countries. This is because all contracts will be effectively denominated in foreign exchange. Further, since the capital markets of developing countries are not well integrated internationally, open floating is likely to result in increased exchange instability.

The other horn of the dilemma is related to the fact that many developing countries took the decision to peg their exchange rates in terms of one or more major currencies. Under the present system of generalized floating, this means that the exchange rates of these countries float against all other currencies to which they are not pegged, so that a fixed exchange rate becomes virtually meaningless under such a system. Under the circumstances, the adoption of the open world price standard still poses critical choices for most developing countries in terms of how to adjust their exchange rates, as well as the currency or basket of currencies to which they should tie the domestic currency. This is further complicated by the fact that, in many cases, official floating is usually synonymous with managed floating of major currencies. This reduces the autonomy and flexibility that can be attached to exchange rate policies of developing countries.

Besides the specific examples given above, adoption of the world price standard can have serious consequences for trade policy and the overall development process. This stems from the fact that it is based on assumptions governing free trade and the operation of market laws domestically and internationally. However, as emphasized earlier, even when investments are chosen according to the free market price standard, many developing countries cannot participate profitably in world trade, and several with a comparative advantage in industrial products fail to achieve their full industrial potential.

This argument should be put in the context of the traditional and continuing debate between "export optimists" and "export pessimists." Trade optimists generally point to the tremendous growth in world trade that has taken place in recent times. Lewis (1980) estimates that it has been growing at about 8 percent per annum in real terms compared to about 0.9 percent per annum between 1913 and 1939, and less than 4 percent between 1873 and 1913. This has been accompanied by notable shifts in the structure of exports of developing countries, with their share of manufactures in total exports increasing from around 8 percent in the 1950s to over 20 percent during the late 1970s.

On the other hand, trade pessimists point out that a relatively few small countries in Asia (South Korea, Taiwan, Hong Kong, Singapore) were primarily responsible for more than 60 percent of this expansion. The majority of developing countries still have to rely on exports of a few primary commodities to developed country markets as the major fuel for their growth engine, and to use Lewis's dictum, there might have been a "slowing down in the engine of growth."

This is related to the general contention that a large majority of developing countries with a potential comparative advantage in industrial products fail to industrialize on a sustained basis because of the unfavorable international environment that they face, and not so much on account of inappropriate domestic pricing standards, such as the pursuit of inward looking strategies.

More fundamentally, supporters of the balanced growth approach to development argue that investment choices based on free trade principles are likely to result in sectoral fragmentation and lopsided development. The tenets of broad-based and balanced development require that the related policies and strategies should aim at achieving optimal consistency among the various sectors of the economy. In this context, the balanced growth approach suggests the necessity for reducing costs and removing various barriers to development, and the creation of various intersectoral demand and supply relationships: backward, forward, technological, and final demand linkages.

For example, the backward linkages would occur when a given economic activity or industry utilizes locally produced intermediate inputs or capital goods. Forward linkages occur when the outputs of such an activity are used as inputs into other industries through various forms of processing. Technological linkages represent a variety of externalities, including the spread of new technologies, methods of organization, infrastructural construction, and so on. The final demand linkages result from the expenditure of factor incomes and taxes paid by an industry.

An interesting technical solution to the conflict between the balanced growth alternative and development based on free trade was proposed by Chenery (1961). He suggested the use of shadow prices within a linear programming framework as a means of reconciling the requisite development objectives with the requirements of optimal resource use. The idea was that such planning models could be used to combine the requirements of balanced growth theory (the interrelationships among various economic activities over the planning horizon) with the need for efficient choice between home production and importing, as well as between the relevant technologies and projects.

The Chenery-type linear planning models are solved mathematically by attaching "weights" or "shadow prices" to various resources and outputs. In essence, these weights or shadow prices behave like market prices in the sense that they change in accordance with the relative scarcity of resources. Further, the shadow prices take on optimal values in equilibrium situations, and in such cases are consistent with balanced growth patterns and comparative advantage.

The technical ingenuity of this approach aside, it raises problems similar to those encountered with any set of optimum prices. It is impossible to define what may be considered to be an optimal set of shadow prices for an economy, and value judgments have to be employed in the choice. One related factor lies in the multiplicity of objectives, usually conflicting, which pricing instruments are meant to serve. A given set of prices and related policies designed to improve efficiency and raise the rate of growth may often conflict with those designed to redistribute incomes. Second, various combinations of policy instruments may be used to achieve the same objective. Third, the lack of homogeneity both within and across economic sectors means that different forms of intervention may be considered appropriate, depending on parameters such as the structure of land ownership and the degree of market segmentation.

Finally, while many policy makers may view prices as unique market-clearing instruments, many economic agents see their value as being politically determined, and therefore normative. Most liberalization programs are based on the assumption that, given an optimal set of prices, most economic agents will behave rationally, thereby assuring the requisite changes in terms of allocative efficiency and growth. However, the ultimate outcome may be heavily influenced by perceptions that are formed about the government in power, such as its arbitrary or capricious behavior, and/or its capacity for political repression.

As one student of the subject notes in the context of Latin American stabilization programs:

> Even a perfectly rational constellation of prices and investment incentives cannot fully convince entrepreneurs that such an edifice will be in place tomorrow. When economic rationality is built upon an arbitrary political regime, which may depend on one general's heartbeat, entrepreneurs will not be easily persuaded that today's relative prices are good predictors of future ones. While the economic team builds policy on the assumption that households and firms behave rationally and process information intelligently, the political team assumes that citizens cannot be trusted to choose their leaders nor to read an uncensored press (Diaz-Alejandro 1981, p. 128).

The Role Of The State

To complete the picture, some brief comments are addressed to the controversial issue concerning the optimal role of the state in economic activity, and the criteria that should be used to delineate the appropriate boundary between the private and the public sector. Choices regarding the desired level of government spending and budget allocations are at the heart of stabilization programs. The usual assumption is that most internal and external imbalances are traceable to excessive government spending and involvement in economic life.

One implication is that the government's role may have to be curtailed, with a greater emphasis to be placed on decentralized planning through the marketplace. Another is that government policies should be redesigned as a means of strengthening the market system. A stronger market system is, in turn, considered to be needed in order to allow public policy to operate more efficiently through the market (Meier 1983, p. 232).

Needless to say, there is no consensus among policy analysts and decision makers about the appropriate role of the state. The orthodox policy framework has been significantly influenced by the neoclassical view of the state's behavior in cooperation with the private sector. From such a perspective, the state expresses individual interests within a broader framework of common purpose. The government therefore becomes an instrument operating for the benefit of the majority, exercising its ability to provide public goods.

In addition, the neoclassical view is that the state has a role in adjusting the allocation of resources in those sectors or industries where there is a divergence between private costs/benefits and social costs/benefits, in alleviating discrepancies between private and public risks, or in public and private time preference through adjustment of interest rates and relative rates of return from investment. Thus, in the neoclassical tradition, the state is seen as a facilitator of private wants and private production. It is supposed to reflect individual preferences within a collective (democratic) framework, as well as organize the collection and disbursement of funds to meet these preferences.

The relevant literature has isolated several cases in which private allocations through the market would not be expected to yield satisfactory results. First, these circumstances could arise in the case of market failure. Instances of such market failure involve the presence of significant economies of scale, externalities, and uncertainties. Such externalities exist when individuals and firms cannot capture the full economic benefits of their investment, and are therefore likely to underinvest from the viewpoint of society. The reverse holds in the case of negative externalities (e.g., river pollution), where the investment imposes costs that he or she does not bear.

Classic cases of market failure include public goods for which it is not easy to charge a market price, or research where externalities may be substantial. In general, public goods include those classes of goods that economic agents must be allowed to consume once these goods are available, irrespective of whether such consuming agents contributed to their production. An example is government expenditure on some of the basic social services discussed earlier.

Public goods also represent particular cases in which government intervention or public investment is justified in their provision. One such is the existence of "natural monopolies" where competitive market activity is prevented for technical reasons. Typical examples are electric power, telephones, and public water supplies. Public sector involvement is also justified in those projects requiring relatively large investments spread over a number of years. In such situations, private short-term returns are usually not high enough to attract the requisite private investment. Further, private investors tend to be more risk-averse compared to government. One reason is that their planning horizon tends to be much shorter than that of the public sector, which is usually based on long-term development plans.

There are also situations in which a need exists to improve the performance of the market. Such situations are exemplified by fragmented capital, labor, or output markets, and the lack of effective communication systems. Accordingly, government involvement may take the form of collecting and distributing various forms of information, as well as monitoring the behavior of markets. In the latter case, the objective is to limit forms of monopolistic behavior such as price fixing, restraints on trade, or organized barriers to entry.

The above decision rules are innocuous enough, and fit neatly into the pro-private enterprise philosophy underlying the orthodox paradigm. Some of the policy implications are straightforward. One is that government involvement in economic activity, either in the form of investment or ownership, should be sanctioned only in those cases where private initiatives could not fulfill the desired tasks. Second, where such involvement takes place, it should be limited to basic industries and infrastructure, leaving the remainder to the private sector. In other words, government investments should help to "relieve pressure" on the private sector by creating a suitable "investment climate," and no attempts should be made to take control of the "commanding heights" of the economy. A third implication is that, since the managerial capacity of the state, especially in developing countries, is limited and at times overextended, uneconomic public enterprises should be liquidated or divested to the private sector.

Any cursory review of recent documents and mission reports would reveal that the above perspectives of thought reflect to some degree current IMF and World Bank philosophy about the appropriate role of the public versus the private sector. Assuming this perception to be correct, questions may be raised about the defensibility of policies based on this approach. The answers to such questions cannot be provided on an a priori basis, and must ultimately depend on the development circumstances facing individual countries, their respective levels of development, and national goals. What can be stated, however, is that policy advice based on the market ideology is an actual and potential source of conflict between many developing countries and international credit agencies.

For example, one such conflict area relates to those sets of government interventions that are aimed, prima facie, at transferring income or power between groups and individuals in the market. Examples include price supports designed to raise farmers' incomes and price controls aimed at protecting the incomes of particular groups of consumers. These practices could be defended if their rationale were purely redistributive. However, there are some instances where such controls are used as political weapons in the overall system of patron–client relationships, or as mechanisms to reduce the role of particular racial, ethnic, or tribal groups in certain forms of economic activity.

Second, it was emphasized earlier that many developing countries may subscribe to national or sector goals other than those dealing with economic efficiency. There are some such cases in which government intervention may be justified on both theoretical and practical policy grounds. A common example is where trade intervention is used as a mechanism to promote the broader goals of development, rather than the more limited ones of free trade and comparative advantage. In this context, trade intervention has been justified on several grounds, including: (1) employment creation; (2) the promotion of self-reliance; (3) terms of trade improvement; (4) infant industry protection, and the related benefits that are likely to accrue from learning by doing, external economies, and technological change; and (5) the need for defense against the effects of foreign trade barriers (Corden 1974). It can also be commented that all countries, developed and developing, attached independent weights to these objectives in their economic or development welfare function.

Finally, an activist role for the state may be envisaged if development is conceptualized as a historical process. In this context, the state can play an entrepreneurial role by participating in a range of economic activities during the earlier stages of development. When development is viewed as a historical process, the state can be considered more as a predecessor to the private sector, rather than as an alternative to it. This may be true even in those cases where state initiatives are socialist in orientation. This is because the outcome of the historical process may be a movement toward forms of capitalist or mixed economic development. This conclusion is suggested by a study of the historical forces underlying the German, French, and Japanese models of economic development.

There is some recognition of this view in World Bank circles. As stated in its *World Development Report 1983*:

> The role of the state changes as the economy does. In least developed countries, the indigenous private sector consists largely of subsistence farmers and small family traders, while the modern sector is dominated by expatriate or minority-owned firms concentrated in a few export crops and mining. Under such circumstances, governments generally feel that they have the resources and the purpose to promote development. In more advanced economies, with the potential for greater private sector activity, the state may play more of a regulatory role, concentrating on rectifying market failures. (World Bank 1983, p. 56)

Bibliography

Anjaria, S. J. et al. 1982. *Developments in International Trade Policy.* Occasional Paper no. 16. Washington, D.C.: International Monetary Fund.

Bacha, Edmar and Lance Taylor. 1971. "Foreign Exchange Shadow Prices: A Critical Review of Current Theories." *Quarterly Journal of Economics* 85:197–224.

Balassa, Bela. 1981. "Adjustment to External Shocks in Developing Countries." World Bank Staff Working Paper no. 472. Washington, D.C.: The World Bank.

Balassa, Bela et al. 1971. *The Structure of Protection in Developing Countries.* Baltimore, MD: Johns Hopkins.

Bautista, Romeo. 1980. "Exchange Rate Adjustment under Generalized Currency Floating: Comparative Analysis among Developing Countries." World Bank Staff Working Paper no. 436. Washington, D.C.: The World Bank.

Bhagwati, Jagdish. 1978. *Foreign Trade Regimes and Economic Development.* Cambridge, MA: Ballinger for the National Bureau of Economic Research.

Bird, Graham. 1979. "IMF Quotas, Conditionality, and the Developing Countries." *ODI Review* 2:56–71.

Blackwell, Carl P. 1978. "Monetary Approach to Balance of Payments Needs Blending with Other Lines of Analysis." *IMF Survey,* February 20, pp. 52–55.

———. 1978a. "Eclectic Approach to Balance of Payments Adjustment Policies and Programs is Too Rigid." *IMF Survey,* March 6, pp. 71–73.

Brandt Commission. 1980. *North–South: A Program for Survival.* Cambridge, MA: MIT Press.

Blitzer, Charles, Peter Clark, and Lance Taylor, eds. 1975. *Economy-Wide Models and Development Planning.* New York: Oxford University.

Chenery, Hollis. 1961. "Comparative Advantage and Development Policy," *American Economic Review* 51:18–51.

Chenery, Hollis et al. 1974. *Redistribution with Growth.* London: Oxford University.

Christensen, Cheryl, and Larry Witucki. 1982. "Food Problems and Emerging Policy Responses in Sub-Saharan Africa." *American Journal of Agrical Economics* 64:889–96.

Cline, William R. 1983. "Economic Stabilization in Developing Countries: Theory and Stylized Facts." In *IMF Conditionality,* edited by John Williamson, 175–208. Washington, D.C.: Institute for International Economics.

Cline, William R., and Sidney Weintraub, eds. 1981. *Economic Stabilization in Developing Countries.* Washington, D.C.: The Brookings Institution.

Coats, Warren L., Jr., and Deena R. Khatkhate. 1980. *Money and Monetary Policy in Less Developed Countries.* New York: Pergamon.

Cooper, Richard N. 1971. *Currency Devaluation in Developing Countries.* Essays in International Finance no. 86, International Finance Section, Department of Economics, Princeton University, Princeton, NJ.

Corden, W. M. 1971. *Theory of Protection.* Oxford: Clarendon.

_____. 1974. *Trade Policy and Economic Welfare.* Oxford: Clarendon.

Crockett, Andrew. 1981. "Stabilization Policies in Developing Countries: Some Policy Considerations." *IMF Staff Papers* 28:54–79.

David, Wilfred L. 1982. "Sugar and Development." Division Working Paper no. 86, Economics and Policy Division, Agriculture and Rural Development Department. Washington, D.C.: The World Bank.

_____. 1984. *Paradigms in Development Thought and Policy.* Washington, D.C.: Horward University. Mimeographed.

David, Wilfred L., and Pasquale Scandizzo. 1980. "Agricultural Growth and Structural Transformation." Division Working Paper no. 30, Economics and Policy Division, Agriculture and Rural Development Department. Washington, D.C.: The World Bank.

Dell, Sidney. 1981. *On Being Grandmotherly: The Evolution of IMF Conditionality.* Essays in International Finance no. 144. International Finance Section, Department of Economics, Princeton University, Princeton, NJ.

_____. 1983. "Stabilization: The Political Economy of the Overkill." In *IMF Conditionality,* edited by John Williamson, 17–46. Washington, D.C.: Institute for International Economics.

Dell, Sidney, and Roger Lawrence. 1980. *The Balance of Payments Adjustment Process in Developing Countries.* New York: Pergamon.

Diaz-Alejandro, Darlos F. 1981. "Southern Cone Stabilization Plans." In *Economic Stabilization in Developing Countries,* edited by William Cline and Sidney Weintraub, 119–47. Washington, D.C.: The Brookings Institution.

Donovan, Donal. 1982. "Macroeconomic Performance and Adjustment under Fund-Supported Programs: The Experience of the 1970s." *IMF Staff Papers* 29:171–203.

Dornbusch, Rudiger. 1980. *Open Economy Macroeconomics.* New York: Basic Books.

Finch, David C. 1983. Adjustment Policies and Conditionalities." In *IMF Conditionality,* edited by John Williamson, 75–86. Washington, D.C.: Institute for International Economics.

Findlay, Ronald. 1973. *International Trade and Development Theory.* New York: Columbia University.

Foxley, Alejandro, and Lawrence Whitehead, eds. 1980. *Economic Stabilization in Latin America: Political Dimensions.* New York: Pergamon.

Frenkel, Jacob and Harry Johnson, eds. 1977. *The Monetary Approach to the Balance of Payments.* Toronto: University of Toronto.

Friedman, Milton, ed. 1956. *Studies in the Quantity Theory of Money.* Chicago, IL: University of Chicago.

_____ . 1969. "The Role of Monetary Policy." In *The Optimum Quantity of Money and Other Essays,* Chapter 5. Chicago, IL: Aldine.

Gold, Joseph. 1979. *Conditionality.* IMF Pamphlet Series no. 31. Washington, D.C.: International Monetary Fund.

Guitián, Manuel. 1981. *Fund Conditionality: Evolution of Principles and Practices.* IMF Pamphlet Series no. 38. Washington, D.C.: International Monetary Fund.

Gurley, John, and Edward Shaw. 1964. *Money in the Theory of Finance.* Washington, D.C.: The Brookings Institution.

Helleiner, Gerald K. 1983. "Lender of Last Resort: The IMF and the Poorest." *American Economic Review* 73:349–53.

International Monetary Fund. 1977. *The Monetary Approach to the Balance of Payments.* Washington, D.C.: International Monetary Fund.

_____ . 1979. "Guidelines to Conditionality." In *Annual Report,* 136–38.

_____ . 1982. *World Economic Outlook.*

_____ . 1982a. *IMF Survey.*

_____ . 1982b. *Articles of Agreement*; reprinted.

_____ . 1983. *Annual Report.*

_____ . 1984. *IMF Survey.*

Johnson, Omotunde. 1974. "Credit Controls as Instruments of Development Policy in the Light of Economic Theory." *Journal of Money, Credit, and Banking* 6:85–99.

_____ . 1976. "The Exchange Rate as an Instrument of Policy in a Developing Country." *IMF Staff Papers* 23:334–48.

Johnson, Omotunde, and Joanne Salop. 1980. "Distributional Aspects of Stabilization Programs in Developing Countries." *IMF Staff Papers* 28:1–23.

Kaldor, Nicholas. 1978. *Further Essays in Applied Economics.* New York: Holmes and Meier.

_____ . 1982. *The Scourge of Monetarism.* New York: Oxford.

_____ . 1983. "Devaluation and Adjustment in Development Countries." *Finance and Development* 20:35–37.

Katseli, Louka T. 1983. "Devaluation: A Critical Appraisal of the IMF's Policy Prescriptions." *American Economic Review* 73:359–63.

Kelly, Margaret R. 1982. "Fiscal Adjustment and Fund-Supported Programs, 1971–80." *IMF Staff Papers* 20:561–602.

Khan, Moshin, and Malcolm D. Knight. 1981. "Stabilization Programs in Developing Countries: Formal Framework." *IMF Staff Papers* 28:1–53.

Killick, Tony, ed. 1982. *Adjustment and Financing in the Developing World: The Role of the International Monetary Fund.* Washington, D.C.: International Monetary Fund and Overseas Development Institute.

Krueger, Anne O. 1974. "The Political Economy of Rent Seeking Society." *American Economic Review* 64:291–303.

_____ . 1978. *Foreign Trade Regimes and Economic Development: Liberalization Attempts and Consequences.* New York: Columbia.

Krugman, Paul, and Lance Taylor. 1978. "Contractionary Effects of Devaluation." *Journal of International Economics* 8:343–82.

Lanyi, Anthony and Rusdu Saracoglu. 1983. "The Importance of Interest Rates in in Developing Countries." *Finance and Development* (International Monetary Fund) 20:20–23.

Lewis, W. Arthur. 1954. "Economic Development with Unlimited Supplies of Labour." *Manchester School of Economic and Social Studies* 23:139–91.

————. 1955. *Theory of Economic Growth.* London: Allen and Unwin.

————. 1980. "The Slowing Down of the Engine of Growth." *American Economic Review* 70:555–64.

————. 1984. "The State of Development Theory." *American Economic Review* 74:1–10.

Little, Ian, Tibor Scitovsky, and Michael Scott. 1970. *Industry and Trade in Some Developing Countries: A Comparative Study.* Oxford: Oxford.

Little, Ian, and James Mirlees. 1974. *Project Appraisal and Planning for Developing Countries.* New York: Basic Books.

Maciejewski, E. B. 1983. " 'Real' Effective Exchange Rates: A Re-Examination of the Major Conceptual and Methodological Issues." *IMF Staff Papers* 30:491–541.

Mansur, A. H. 1983. "Determining the Appropriate Levels of Exchange Rates for Developing Economies." *IMF Staff Papers* 30:784–814.

McKinnon, Ronald I. 1973. *Money and Capital in Economic Development.* Washington, D.C.: The Brookings Institution.

————. 1981. "The Exchange Rate and Macroeconomic Policy: Changing Postwar Perceptions." *Journal of Economic Literature* 19:531–57.

Meier, Gerald M., ed. 1983. *Pricing Policy for Development Management.* Baltimore, MD: Johns Hopkins.

Nashashibi, Karim. 1983. "Devaluation in Developing Countries: The Difficult Choices." *Finance and Development* 20:14–17.

Nugent, Jeffrey, and Pan Yotopolous. "What Has Orthodox Development Economics Learned from Recent Experience?" *World Development* 7:541–54.

Nurske, Ragnar, 1953. *Problems of Capital Formation in Developing Countries.* New York: Oxford.

Pyatt, Graham, and Allan R. Roe. 1979. *Social Accounting For Development Planning, with Special Reference to Sri Lanka.* Cambridge: Cambridge

Pyatt, Graham, and Erik Thorbecke. 1976. *Planning Techniques for a Better Future.* Genèva: International Labour Office.

Reichmann, Thomas, and Richard Stillson. 1978. "Experience with Programs of Balance of Payments Adjustment: Stand-by Arrangements in the Higher Tranches, 1963–72." *IMF Staff Papers* 25:293–309.

Reynolds, Clark. 1969. "Achieving Greater Financial Independence for Latin America." *World Development* 3:839–40.

Rhomberg, Rudolph R. 1976. "Indices of Effective Exchange Rates." *IMF Staff Papers* 23:88–112.

Schumpeter, Joseph A. 1949. "Science and Ideology." *American Economic Review* 39:345–59.

———. 1978. *History of Economic Analysis.* New York: Oxford.

Sen, Amartya K. 1961. "On Optimising the Rate of Saving." *Economic Journal* 71:479–98.

Shaw, Edward S. 1973. *Financial Deepening and Economic Development.* New York: Oxford.

Sheahan, John. 1980. "Market Oriented Economic Policies and Political Repression in Latin America." *Economic Development and Cultural Change* 28:267–92.

Solomon, Robert. 1977. *The International Monetary System, 1945–76: An Insider's View.* New York: Harper and Row.

Stern, Ernest. 1983. "World Bank Financing of Structural Adjustment." In *IMF Conditionality,* edited by John Williamson, 87–107. Washington, D.C.: Institute for International Economics.

Streeten. Paul P. 1974. "Social Science Research on Development: Some Problems in the Use and Transfer of an Intellectual Technology." *Journal of Economic Literature* 12:1290–1300.

———. 1981. *Development Perspectives.* New York: St. Martins.

———. 1982. *First Things First: Meeting Basic Human Needs.* New York: Oxford.

Taylor, Lance. 1979. *Macro Models for Developing Countries.* New York: McGraw-Hill.

———. 1981. "IS/LM in the Tropics: Diagrammatics of the New Structuralist Macro Critique." In *Economic Stabilization in Developing Countries,* edited by William Cline and Sidney Weintraub, 465–506. Washington, D.C.: The Brookings Institution.

Thoburn, John T. 1977. *Primary Commodity Exports and Economic Development.* New York: John Wiley.

Timbergen, Jan. 1976. *RIO: Reshaping the International Order: A Report to the Club of Rome.* New York: E. P. Dutton.

United Nations Research Institute for Social Development (UNRISD). 1980. *The Quest for a Unified Approach to Development.* Geneva: UNRISD.

Valdés, Alberto, and Joachim Zietz. 1980. *Agricultural Protection in OECD Countries: Its Cost to Less Developed Countries.* Washington, D.C.: International Food Policy Research Institute.

Wai, U Tun. 1972. *Financial Intermediation and National Savings in Developing Countries.* New York: Praeger.

Wilber, Charles K., ed. 1973. *The Political Economy of Development and Underdevelopment.* New York: Random House.

Williamson, John, ed. 1983. *IMF Conditionality.* Washington, D.C.: Institute for International Economics.

_____ . 1983a. "On Seeking to Improve IMF Conditionality." *American Economic Review* 73:354–8.

World Bank. 1975. *Rural Development Sector Policy Paper.*

_____ . 1975a. *The Assault on World Poverty.* Baltimore: Johns Hopkins.

_____ . 1981. *Accelerated Development in Sub-Saharan Africa: An Agenda for Action.* Washington, D.C.: The World Bank.

_____ . 1981a. *World Development Report.* New York: Oxford.

_____ . 1983. *World Development Report.* New York: Oxford.

_____ . 1984. *World Development Report.* New York: Oxford.

_____ . 1984a. *Toward Sustained Development in Sub-Saharan Africa: A Joint Program of Action.* Washington, D.C.: The World Bank.

Index

Absorption, domestic, 36–39; and income, 34–36. *See also* balance of payments

Adjustment, burden, 97–99; processes, 19–29; and supply rigidities, 106–108. *See also* balance of payments; interest rate; exchange rate

Balance of payments, disequilibria, 4, 14–15, 25–26; monetary approach to, 54–56; and external environment, 98–106. *See also* debt

Capital, accumulation and savings, 7, 48–51; markets, 37, 71, 80; scarcity of, 58, 81; opportunity cost of, 80. *See also* savings; investment

Credit, policies, 77–78; tranches, 18–21; domestic, 38–51. *See also* government; debt

Debt, crisis, 103–106; service, 104

Devaluations, nominal, 91; monetary approach to, 88–89; effects of, 91–94

Development, goals and instruments, 107, 115–117; and conditionality, 118–120; balanced growth approach to, 125–126. *See also* World Bank

Employment, full, 57; and parallel economy, 73–74. *See also* inflation; development; income

Exchange rate, policies, 91–94; overvaluation, 71, 83; nominal and effective, 85–86; in Africa, 86; equilibrium, 80–82, 91

Exports, earning instability, 101. *See also* trade

Government, budget and expenditure, 34–36; role of, 127–130; institutions, 76–77; intervention, 77–82; transfers and income distribution, 129

Imports, structure of, 89–90; restrictions and rent seeking, 72. *See also* trade

Income, distribution, 113; and devaluation, 93; real, 15, 93

Inflation, rate of, 3, 4, 27; and employment tradeoff, 53, 59; and money supply, 53–54

Interest rate, policy, 77–79; law of one, 57–58; investment, savings, consumption, 78–80; floating and variable, 104; shadow, 80–81

International Monetary Fund (IMF), quotas, 15–18; conditionality, 22–24; lending resources, 13–19; and development, 7–8, 110

About the Author

WILFRED L. DAVID is a Graduate Professor of Economics and African Studies at Howard University, Washington, D.C. Until 1977 he was Professor and Chairman of the Economics Department at Fisk University, Nashville, Tennessee. He has also held academic appointments at Vanderbilt University, the University of Delaware, and Brooklyn College of the City University of New York. He has served for many years as a consultant to the World Bank where he was also a former staff member.

Dr. David has published widely in the area of international economic development. His articles and reviews have appeared in the *American Economic Review, World Development, Finance and Development,* and the London *Financial Times.*

Dr. David holds a B.A. with honors in economics and philosophy from the University of London, and a D.Phil. from the University of Oxford, England.